Guide to 50

Interesting and Mysterious

Sites

in the Mojave

Volume 2

by William Jack Mann
A.K.A. Shortfuse

Shortfuse Publishing Co.

Barstow, California

Guide to 50 Interesting and Mysterious Sites in the Mojave

Volume 2

by William Jack Mann

Shortfuse Publishing Co.

30 Hilltop Terrace

Barstow, CA 92311

USA

©1999 by William J. Mann

All Rights Reserved

Second Printing June 2002

Set in 11 point Times Roman type

Book Design and Layout by Ron McKinley

Southwest Savvy

Apple Valley, CA

Cover Design by Dave Tisthammer

thegraphicguy.com

Cover photograph of author taken

inside the Lava Tube

by Ron McKinley

ISBN 0-9667947-1-0

Dedication

I am dedicating this book to my best friend, buddy, lover, mother of my son and four daughters, Dottie Mann. I call her my child bride because she was nineteen when we married. For forty-five years, it has been a wild ride through life in both good and bad times. I almost lost her in a terrible accident in 1986, that left her handicapped and in a wheelchair, but it didn't dampen her spirit. We still have a good quality of life and enjoy every day together. It was a good day when she came into my life. I wouldn't know what to do without her.

Preface

I have camped, prospected and led tours into the back country of the Mojave Desert for over fifty years. My cousin, Ron Brubaker, and I co-founded a small mining company and never dreamed it would still be in business fifty years later.

In the early years, we were struggling to make ends meet, so we took on the distributorship of the Hercules Powder Co. In the 1950's, there was an enormous amount of small mining and prospecting still going on. Being interested in history, archeology and mining, I met most of these colorful characters involved in mining and listened to their stories and sometimes prospected with them to learn as much as I could about the desert.

We sold and delivered explosives throughout the desert. Many of these sites were selected as a result of our travels and experiences. On weekends, with the family, I would explore these areas. Dottie and I raised five children this way.

The desert is a huge, awesome, and beautiful place but can be unforgiving and cruel if a person is careless. For example, three years ago a German family of four took a two-wheel-drive vehicle into a remote area of Death Valley in July, got stuck, and paid a horrible price for their mistake. Only their van with three flat tires was found. To this day, they are still missing. I would not want anyone to get into trouble using this book, so take the "Warning by Shortfuse" very seriously. This book is meant as a guide for the back-country enthusiast. The directions are as complete as I can give and the mileage is approximate but should get you within visual range of the site. Don't be in a hurry looking for these sites. You may even find some I have missed. I am still finding great places. I know there are more. I hope you enjoy this book and develop the love that I have for the desert.

I have used the DeLorme Southern and Central California Atlas and Gazetteer as a reference as it is readily available throughout the state. I used the abbreviation: "S & C DeLorme" throughout the book. Also, the different sites are grouped by area: Newberry Springs, Baker, Shoshone-Tecopa, Turquoise Mountain, Valley Wells and Mountain Pass. If you start exploring in one area you can visit all the sites in that area as the directions are progressive. GPS readings were taken using the NAD 27 CONUS standard.

Road conditions, naturally, are subject to change. Be very careful when travelling in the desert right after a rain.

Follow the rock cairns. I have tried to put up rock cairns at key spots to keep you on the right track. I have put up so many rock cairns that my friends are starting to call me "Rock Pile Bill." It is fun!

Now for some definitions:

Arrastré – primitive system of grinding ore. Big boulders were assembled in a circle and usually a mule or burro was used to drag a heavy rock around the circle filled with ore to crush it. Later on steam engines performed this chore and later gasoline engines dragged rocks or heavy pieces of metal to crush the ore.

Metaté and mono – metaté is a hard, smooth, rock slab used for grinding seed and grain. After a lot of use it becomes hollowed out like a shallow bowl. The mono is a rock used for grinding the seed or grain against the metaté. This system is still in use among primtive peoples.

Mortar and pestle – mortar is a bowl carved into heavy rock, usually bedrock, and the pestle is used by hand to grind grain or seeds into flower or meal within the mortar. Mortar and pestle is more common in the foothills and the mountains than in the desert.

Cairns – a pile of rocks used by Indians and pioneers to mark a trail. "Rock Pile Bill" used this system throughout the book to mark roads and trails for you.

Acknowledgements

I have many people to thank in producing volume 2. It has been fun and Dottie and I have made many new friends and have drawn closer to our older friends. Ron and Kandee McKinley continue to amaze me with their talent. Without them, there would be no book. Thanks to Dave Tisthammer of *thegraphicguy.com* for the wonderful cover.

I have Don Taylor to thank for all the hours and miles he has put in. He has taken hundreds of pictures and I lean on him a great deal. He makes trips fun and is always ready to go.

Don Putnam is always ready to go and now has a new wife, Myrtie, who fits right in. Both of them have great humor and make the trips fun.

Much of the success of volume 1 is due to the cartoons of Rocky Johnson. Thanks a lot, Rocky, for all the hours you spent on volume 2. All cartoons in this book are by Rocky Johnson.

Phil and Leann Benton are generous with their time and talents. Not only have they made the trips fun, but have taken hundreds of photos. I still cannot believe that Phil and Don Taylor drove over 100 miles one way, to retrieve my beloved prospector's staff that I left at the Sagamore Mine. I will never forget Leann as the spacewoman from Uranus when we camped at David's Cross and were expecting the UFO's to land! They never appeared but we had a great time waiting for them!

Thanks to Dennis Casebier for providing pictures and information. I admire him greatly.

Gary Wilson has been a great help with the GPS readings . He has taken pictures and made the beautiful display holders for the book.

Tim Read, Sally Cunkleman and their staff of the BLM in Barstow have been very helpful. Gina Robison of the BLM went on trips and took pictures. She is a delight to be around. Mary Martin and her staff of the National Park Service have also been helpful.

I have been encouraged by Bill Tomlinson, Neal Johns, George and Patty Jones and other friends in the Mojave River Valley Museum. Thanks to Sonny and Jean Hansen for the help and pictures.

Mike McCain flew me over sites, took pictures of the rattlesnake and cactus flowers.

Harvey Wilkins took the great picture of the tarantula. Lara Hartley took the picture of the Forks in the Road gang. Carlos Gallinger was very helpful in showing me sites and going with me into the back country.

Gene and Bev Stoops make things happen. They are fun and a joy to be around. Gene took the great picture of the sun shining through the Shamans Eye.

I want to thank Lois Clark for information on the Grand Canyon of the Tecopa where she lived as a child.

Thanks to Susan Sorrells for her time in showing me sites and encouraging me to do the Shoshone-Tecopa area. Thanks to her brother, Charles, for giving us permission to cross his property to get to Twelve Mile Spring.

Thanks to Brian and Bonnie Brown of China Ranch for their help. I admire them greatly. Joe Pizzatola has also been a great help.

Thanks to Bernie Kerkvilet for the pictures of the edible and useful plants of the Mojave included in this volume. Bernie has a B.S. degree in ornamental horticulture from Cal State Poly-Pomona and has been a landscape contractor in the San Bernardino mountains for more than 24 years. He has been studying edible plants for over 28 years and currently teaches on the subject through Cal State San Bernardino.

I want to thank my daughter, Julie Mann Clemmer, for handling the credit card sales and her husband and my son-in-law, Bob Clemmer, for setting up dealers across the desert to handle the book.

Last, but not least, I want to thank my wife and buddy of many years, Dottie, for the hours she spent typing and proof reading my work and putting up with me while this project was in progress. Without her, there would not have been a book.

WARNING!!

Traveling unprepared in the vast Mojave Desert could be hazardous to your health. Please read the following instructions before venturing out into the great unknown.

Old Mine Shafts. The Mojave Desert is a treasure trove of almost every mineral and gemstone known. It has been mined heavily for about two hundred years. It is filled with thousands of mine shafts that beckon to be explored. DON'T! If you want to climb down, be sure you have a stout rope around you and held by a strong person who belongs to the same political party! I don't recommend that this person be your mother-in-law! If you still insist on climbing down old mine shafts, okay, because Barstow has a good search and rescue squad that needs practice retrieving bodies from mine shafts.

Rattlesnakes. I carry a snake stick and keep it ahead of me at all times. I have been struck at numerous times and even chased by a mean sidewinder! Yes, they can spring clear off the ground. It is amazing how agile you can be when one is hot on your posterior. The hotter it is, the meaner they are. The sidewinder should be the logo for the IRS! Seriously, you should always be careful where you put your hands and feet. If struck, head for the nearest hospital, keeping the area as cold as possible. Snakebite kits are still sold but the best recommendation is to get to a hospital as quick as you can.

Weather. Disregard all weather forecasts. Dad Fairbanks, the famous rancher and miner from Shoshone and Greenwater, said years ago that anyone who tries to predict the weather in the desert is either a greenhorn or a damn fool. Be prepared for everything. If you get into a cloudburst or sandstorm, don't be surprised. It is not a disaster if you are prepared. It is an adventure! I have never had a disaster on the desert, but plenty of adventures!

Water. When you go into the back country make sure you have plenty of water, cold beer and a bag of bones. In the early days I carried a bag of carrots too. People who live in isolated areas are usually not very friendly. They are out there for a reason. The common medium of exchange is beer. I have been greeted with a cold stare by a gun-toting hermit and was once greeted by a shot overhead. Without a word, I reach into my ice chest and handed over a cold beer. In this way, I make life-long friends of desert characters. They always have at least one dog. I toss Rover a couple of bones and we are buddies for life. Surprisingly, the burro is still present. He is a prized companion and friend so I give him a carrot. They all have good memories and it is fun to drive up the second time and see the old prospector, dog, and the burro start salivating at the same time when they recognize me. As of 1997, Green Turtle Jim at Keeler has two burros as friends and companions. He has trained them to fetch, roll- over and sit up. He kept a baby book on them from birth. They used to sleep with him in his bed until they got too big. I think their names are Sweet Pea and Petunia. By the way, if you get marooned in the desert and run out of water, you can party on the beer and chew on the bones and the carrots! This is called survival.

Compatible Traveling Companion. Always have a second vehicle besides the usual cell phone, tools and camping gear. Make sure each vehicle has plenty of gas and enough food and water to survive several days if need be. (If both vehicles break down, you can party on the beer and survive on the bones and carrots. Heck! You may not want to be rescued!

How Shortfuse Got His Name

In the early years of our business, both Ron Brubaker and I had blasting licenses. When we started in 1950, the rock business was slow getting started so we took all sorts of odd jobs to keep food on the table. Some of these jobs included blasting. People who did blasting were scarce on the high desert so we were asked to do all kinds of jobs. For example, I blew up two railroad bridges and fortunately got the right ones; blasted set-up concrete inside redi-mix trucks; broke up concrete inside buildings; shot numerous wells to shake up the scale on the intake valves and many other jobs.

One of the jobs using dynamite was to carefully shake-up the concrete on an arrastré that the Mojave River Valley Museum was relocating from an isolated gold mine. This included many small blasts using timed fuses. There were many movie cameras trained on the blast site. The blasts went off before I said they would and the cameramen were annoyed. Someone said, "We'll just call you 'Shortfuse' from now on." The name stuck and then they started calling my wife, Dottie, "Dynamite", and that name stuck too. Anyway, it has been fun.

Contents

Turquoise Mountain Area

Valley Wells Area

Mountain Pass Area

BATTLE OF BLACK BUTTE

Newberry Springs Area

Black Butte is an enormous pile of black lava that rose through a weak spot in the earth's crust. It is a famous landmark that could be seen for a long distance by travelers from either direction. It is on the level surrounded by sand dunes and playas which indicates water and game. It was a favorite camping site for both historic and pre-historic man and remains a good camping spot to this day.

The last confrontation between Indians and settlers in this area occurred here. It is called the Battle of Black Butte but was more a skirmish than a battle.

Black Butte as seen from across the old Highway 66. Photos by Don Taylor.

The Indians lived mostly in the mesquite clumps and sand dunes adjoining the playa south of Black Butte. The south side or playa is the most spectacular. A great place to explore.

Directions: Exit I-40 at Newberry Springs off-ramp; go through the small community of Newberry Springs to Newberry Road 1.8 miles and turn left onto Black Butte Road at 2.4 miles. At 3.9 miles turn left along a fence line. It is .6 miles to Black Butte, 4.5 miles total.
Location: S&C De Lorme, page 82, B-3
Coordinates: N34° 51" 15.9', W116° 41' .583', elevation:1786' ± 138'
Vehicle: 2WD

Scenic sand dunes across the highway from Black Butte.

IMMIGRANT POINT

Newberry Springs Area

Immigrant Point is at the end of a point of rocks that juts out into the Mojave River Valley from the Newberry Mountains just east of the small town of Newberry Springs. There was a large spring and riparian area there complete with huge cottonwood trees and wild grapevines. Some pioneer put a well down and to his surprise the water rose on its own, thus becoming an artesian well. Before settlers came, the Indians used this spot for hundreds of years to camp and hunt for food. On the point approximately 150 feet from the sand, they left a perfect bedrock mortar for all to see and enjoy. The ground around the point for hundreds of feet is black from the fires of these Indians and the travelers that followed them. The wagon trains used to camp and rest in this area. If they were coming from the east they would have had a long haul without good water and forage.

Immigrant Point is the low hill on the left approaching from the west. Photos by Don Taylor.

Just east of here is an underground dike or fault that cuts off the water and keeps it from flowing eastward underground. The first name of the community was simply called "Water." For years, the railroad has hauled water from Newberry to points east. The water table has fallen largely due to the many alfalfa ranches but you can still see the top of the old concrete cistern and the trunk of an old cottonwood tree. The well was still flowing in the 1950's when I arrived on the desert and it is still a great pleasure to explore.

Try to visualize all of the activity that went on around this point of rocks. The name came from the many immigrants that were on wagon trains traveling across the country. If you climb this point of rocks, you get a great view of the Mojave River Valley and see a little of the original Highway 66 as it skirts the hills. Just down from the top of Immigrant Point on the west side of the first ledge of rock is a delightful panel of petroglyphs. These were pecked into the rock many hundreds, if not thousands, of years ago by some Indian artist. What was he trying to say? We probably will never know but what I do know is that he left a precious legacy for us to ponder and enjoy. Please do not touch or disturb them so others can enjoy them also.

Directions: Exit I-40 at Newberry Springs off-ramp and go 1.0 miles. Turn left on dirt road immediately after you have gone through a small cut in the highway. Go to the end of the road—about .1 mile).

Location: S&C De Lorme, page 82, B-3

Coordinates: N34° 49' 40.7", W116° 40' .329', elevation 1841'

Vehicle: 2WD

View of the playa where the old cistern was located. Photo by Don Taylor.

Leave Us Alone!

View looking west from the top of Immigrant Point along Old Highway 66. Photos by Don Taylor.

WELCOME TO
DEATH
VALLEY

The author points out a bedrock metaté. Photo by Don Taylor.

FORKS IN THE ROAD
Hawley Mill and Way Station Sites

Newberry Springs Area

Forks in the Road is the meeting of two very important and historic wagon roads. They were used from the 1860s until the railroads took over about the turn of the century. The Mojave Road comes from the east and meets the Mormon Road from Salt Lake City, Utah. This is similar to present day Barstow where two roads join: I-15 from Salt Lake and I-40 from points east. The pioneers from Salt Lake had it especially hard because the last two major springs—Bitter Springs and Salt Springs—consisted of very poor, brackish water. I have tasted the water at both of these springs and wonder how these poor people and animals survived. The cool, sweet water of the Mojave River must have been a welcome sight to both man and beast. The Mojave River Valley also had good forage and game most of the time. It was a great place to rest from the rigors of the trail.

A short distance to the west was the mill and way station of Isaac Hawley. Hawley established his way station in 1874 to furnish supplies and repairs to the wagons of the travelers crossing the desert. He maintained a blacksmith shop much like our present day garages. He closed in 1889.

I marvel at the toughness and fortitude of these people. They are the ones that made this country the great country that it is today! A great site to explore.

Directions: Exit I-15 at Minneola Road east of Yermo and go south across both Yermo Road and the railroad tracks .6 miles to Calico Blvd. Turn left, continue straight at 1.1 miles and follow old fence line, continue straight at 1.3 miles. At 1.4 miles, Hawley's Mill site is approximately one hundred yards south in the rubble area. Continue on the

The author and a group from the MRVM stand in the Forks of the Road. Photo by Lara Hartley.

road to 2.0 miles and Forks in the Road is thirty to fifty yards to the north. Look for my cairns.

Location: S&C De Lorme, page 82, A-3
Coordinates: N35° 54' .625', elevation 1809±
Vehicle: High clearance 2WD

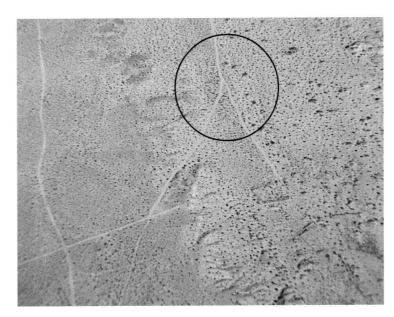

Aerial view of Forks in the Road. Photo by Beth Pinnell.

Indian Paint Brush (*Castilleja Spp.*) Can be red, pink, yellow or white. What appears to be the flowers are actually bracts. The actual flower is inside the covering of the bracts. Both bracts and flowers can be eaten raw. There is a bit of sweet nectar at the end of the flowers' corolla tube. Indian Paint Brush tends to absorb selenium so care should be taken not to over do it in areas where selenium is present in the soil.

F-4 PHANTOM CRASH SITE

Newberry Springs Area

On New Year's Day, 1964, a Navy F-4 jet was flying in the vicinity of the "Sleeping Beauty". The Sleeping Beauty is an extension of the Cady Mountains that resembles a woman sleeping on her back. Something went wrong, but the pilot safely ejected. The plane came in at a low angle and very fast. It hit in a level, sandy area and scooped out a crater and threw wreckage over a large area. The plane literally disintegrated into small pieces which are lying everywhere. The impact is an awesome study of extreme violence. Use care, many of the pieces are very sharp. Please don't remove anything from this interesting site so others can enjoy it.

The author standing among the wreckage of the F-4 Phantom. Photos by Don Taylor.

Directions: Exit I-40 at Hector off-ramp east of Newberry Springs. Turn east on old Highway 66 and go 8.4 miles to Pisgah Crater Road. Turn left and go under I-40 and immediately turn left on a road that runs past a large water tank and a row of trees. This road runs along the railroad tracks and in about .5 mile (8.9) you will come to the crossing. Use care,

some trains are very fast. After crossing, turn right and go to the powerline access road and stay on it for 3.0 miles (11.9). You will pass a sign that says "100." Look for my cairn at the mouth of a wash. Turn left up the wash for .7 miles (12.6) and at another of my cairns on your left, hike out of the wash. In about 200 yards you will see the wreckage scattered over a large area.

Location: S&C De Lorme page 83, B-5.5

Coordinates: N34° 46' 42.5", W116° 19' .023', elevation: 2520' ±

Vehicle: 4WD

MIDWAY STATION

Baker Area

Photograph of the portrait of E. B. Failing that hangs in the Bun Boy restaurant in Baker. Photo by Ron McKinley.

Around 1920, E. B. Failing and his wife, Hazel, left Wisconsin in their family Buick and headed for California. They had heard stories of the good life and pleasant weather and decided to go and seek their fortune. E.B. was very mechanical and liked to work on all things mechanical. On the dirt road called Highway 91, 35 miles northeast of Barstow, the old Buick "gave up the ghost". It was a major breakdown in a remote area of the Mojave Desert. In 1920, when you broke down, you were stuck there and camped out until you could get the parts and get running again. This was usually days and in some cases, weeks. E. B. sent for the parts and put up a tent to shelter his family. It wasn't long before other travelers limped in with various problems and E.B. was in the garage business. Water was hauled from Afton Canyon. Gasoline was brought in by the barrel. Hazel served food to the stranded and soon found herself managing a roadside cafe.

Business boomed and the Failings expanded. A tow truck was needed, so he converted the old Buick into a tow truck. In between repair jobs, E. B. built more permanent quarters out of railroad ties. Shelter was needed for the stranded tourists, so he built four sturdy cabins for their comfort just across Highway 91 to the south. Electricity was needed, so a generator was installed. Soon Midway was selected as a bus stop. When asked where his station was located, he would say it was about midway between Barstow and Baker, and the name stuck. In 1927, the family moved to Baker, and built a station where the Mad Greek now stands. The Failings are one of the true pioneer families of the Mojave Desert. An oil painting of E. B. hangs in the Bun Boy Restaurant in Baker. It is because of their hard work and dedication that others were inspired to create this great country of ours!

The first Midway has long been bypassed and abandoned and nothing remains but slabs and debris with lots of memories. Thanks to Bill and Joan Best and Leann Benton for this delightful story of trials and tribulations of their ancestors. A great place to explore.

Directions: Exit I-15 at Afton offramp, turn right or south, and immediately turn right again on the paved access road. Pavement ends at 2.6 miles, stay on the dirt road and at 2.8 miles turn right on old Hwy 91 (some pavement still shows). At 3.3 miles go straight, and at 4.0 miles look for slabs and debris on the right. This is the old midway station and complex.
Location: S&C De Lorme, page 69, D-5
Coordinates: N35° 01' .952', W116° 27' .750', elevation1779' ± 103'
Vehicle: High Clearance 2WD

EMERGENCY, EMERGENCY!
Baker CAP Field

Baker Area

North of Baker, on Highway 127, on the south shore of Silver Lake, is an abandoned airfield and if you look closely to your left, you will be surprised to see among the foundations and slabs, a rectangular swimming pool. This is the ruins and site of a World War II Civil Air Patrol training base and airfield. This was also the site for navigation light beacons used by the

Author beside the old swimming pool. All photos of this site by Ron McKinley.

early airmail pilots on their run from Los Angeles to Las Vegas to Salt Lake City and beyond. It was also an emergency military landing strip. I have a personal interest in this site, because in 1943 and 1944, I was in the Pomona Civil Air Patrol. Due to WWII restrictions, private planes could not be flown within one hundred miles of the coast so we came from Pomona to Silver Lake to train. We used the lake as the airfield and taxied to the buildings after each training session.

One day we were on the field and a radio order came for us to clear the field because a squadron of B.T.s (basic trainers from the Army Air Corps) were coming in for an emergency landing. We cleared the field just in time for ten or twelve planes to make a landing. The pilots skidded to a stop, jumped out, and

Broken pieces of the lenses from the old light beacons that guided early air mail pilots.

ran for the head. Evidently, they ate something for breakfast that didn't agree with them and the urge hit them all at the same time! This was the emergency!

When the base closed after the war some of the buildings were moved to Baker and are still standing.

This is a large area of ruins and fun to explore. I can shut my eyes and hear the engines roar and those poor pilots running for the toilets. Spend some time here, wander over the site, then close your eyes and imagine what went on here so many years ago. Yes, Shortfuse was here.

Directions: Exit I-15 at Baker and turn north on SH127. At 5.0 miles you'll see a call box on the left. At 5.6 miles turn left and you'll see the ruins of an old swimming pool. Park and explore.
Location: S&C DeLorme, pg. 70, B-1
Coordinates: N35° 20' .572', W116° 05' 00", elevation: 1311' ± 190'
Vehicle: 2WD

The author beside the ruins of the old operations building.

Ruins of the old control tower.

SILVER LAKE

Baker Area

Silver Lake was an important supply center for the mines and mining communities in the area. It was at the crossroads of several important wagon roads. It gained importance when the Tonapah and Tidewater Railroads arrived there in 1906. People could get on the railroad at Silver Lake, transfer at Ludlow, and go into the Los Angeles area. Roads in the area were very primitive and with the coming of the railroad, it really stimulated the area. With the shut-down of Greenwater, Tiger Lil moved her "hotel" to Silver Lake. Silver Lake had a post office and a newspaper called the "Miner". Originally built on the surface of the dry lake, it was moved to higher ground after the wet year of 1915. Silver Lake got its name from the silver, shimmering reflection of the dry lake in the summer afternoons. There are ruins scattered

Ruins of old adobe building. All photos of this site by Ron McKinley.

over a large area of desert east of the lake. The white piles of talc scattered along the road are left from trucks that were too heavy. There was a public scale located here and the truckers would check their loads after loading at the mines. If they were overloaded, they would dump the excess.

Silver Lake Cemetery was used for many years and is in fact, still being used. Look to the north from the talc piles and you will see the fenced cemetery. unfortunately, most of the markers from the old graves have disappeared but the mounds are still there. The more recent burials are well marked. Please let these pioneers rest in peace!

There are literally hundreds of

Silver Lake cemetery north of the adobe ruins.

acres that need to be explored. Have fun but look out for the ghosts of Silver Lake!

Directions: Exit I-15 at Baker and go north on SH127. At 8.3 miles you'll see the adobe ruins of the old settlement of Silver Lake. Approximately 300 yards to the NW you'll see the old cemetery.
Location: S&C DeLorme, pg. 70, B-1
Coordinates: N35° 22' .283', W116° 06' .824', elevation: 1344' ± 492'
Vehicle: 2WD

Another view of the adobe ruins.

SHAMAN'S EYE IN THE SKY

Baker Area

The Shaman's Eye in the Sky is a gigantic volcanic neck rising hundreds of feet out of the desert floor. A volcanic neck is the solidified column of lava left after a volcano dies. The softer material on the outside erodes away leaving a shaft or tower. The Devil's Tower in Wyoming is a perfect example. Usually a volcanic neck is round as most of the vents are round. In this case the lava must have come up through the earth's crust through a large crack, because this column is long and narrow like a large slab. It almost looks like a large hand sticking out of the desert. What is most unusual is that in the middle of the hand is a large hole five or six feet in diameter. In the late afternoon, the slab casts a long shadow over the desert and as the sun sinks lower an eye appears in the shadow and moves over the desert picking up speed as the sun sets. When the sun drops behind the horizon the eye dashes across the last few hundred feet of hills and vanishes. It is an awesome site but has to be timed just perfectly to get the best effect. The sun moves around and only shines directly through the eye for a short period of time. The first time I saw it was in December a week after the winter solstice (December 22) and we saw the whole eye move across the desert. Three weeks later, we saw only part of the eye move. At sunrise, the process is reversed.

As I started on this book I ran into an old friend who is part Indian. This man has spent years in these desert mountains and has shown me some incredible sites. He is a professional tracker and big horn sheep guide as well as an avid naturalist and amateur archeologist. I told him I was writing Volume II and asked him if he knew of any unusual sites in this area. He hesitated a long time and then told me the location and story of the Shaman's Eye in the Sky. He said: "Legend has it that the great Shaman of the Sky came down through this eye and created mankind." He continued, "It's alleged to be a very sacred area and I am convinced they held ceremonies here at certain times of the year. I have looked for the ceremonial sites but never found any—but I'm still searching." He gave me permission to publish this site but under no circumstances am I to reveal his name. He said, "If the ghosts of my ancestors find out that I revealed this site they will come for me." Enjoy this mysterious and unusual spot and experience the reverence that I have for it. It is listed on some maps as Sawtooth.

Directions: Exit I-15 at Baker and turn south on Kelbaker Road. At 5.8 miles turn left on a road that stretches "straight as string" and go 11.6 miles. The gigantic volcanic neck on your right with the hole near the top is the Shaman's Eye in the Sky. The corrals with the water tanks that you pass halfway there is Henry Springs.
Location: S&C DeLorme, page 70, B-3
Coordinates: N35° 22' .351', W115° 48' .310', elevation 4019' ± 183'
Vehicle: High clearance 2WD

Similar view as the one on the next page but at a different time of year. Photo by Ron McKinley.

Near sunset at the Shaman's Eye during late December and early January each year. Photo by Gene Stoops.

Sun streaming through the Shaman's Eye onto group from the Mojave River Valley Museum. Photo by Gene Stoops.

A slightly different angle of the one shown earlier. Photo by Gene Stoops.

Rare albino rattler photographer by Mike McCain near the Shaman's Eye.

INDIAN SPRINGS SHAMAN'S CAVE

Baker Area

Indian Springs is actually a series of springs and seeps along a wash system for approximately ½ mile. You reach the end of the road and a small, dry waterfall.

There is a large turn around area to park or camp in. Remember Shortfuse says to never camp in the bottom of a dry wash because a flash flood could prove to be disastrous.

After you hike over the small waterfall, look up to your left and you will see an old trail leading up the side of the canyon to a large rock shelter which is the Shaman's Cave.

Leann Benton and I built a large cairn at the start of this trail to help you find the

The road ends here in front of the Shaman's Cave. The cave is located near the top on the left side. Photos by Don Taylor.

Shaman's Cave. Beautiful barrel cactus are growing out of the rocks. My anonymous native American tracker and guide friend told me that as local legend has it this is where the Shaman came to perform healing rites and that squaws and children were not allowed in this sacred place. There are some beautiful petroglyphs here including a nice one of a snake. The large wash system in this area is called Indian Creek. As you hike up this beautiful wash, look on both sides and up some of the tributaries and you will be rewarded with many petroglyphs. Some of these panels are outstanding.

The scenery is spectacular, especially in the spring, when the flowers and cactus are blooming. This is also big horn sheep and wild burro country. You can see where they and coyotes have dug numerous holes in the bottom of the wash to get water. On your way into Indian Springs, about halfway there, look to your left about 150 yards and you will see mine ruins including the walls of a delightful stone cabin. Remember, take nothing but pictures, leave nothing but footprints!

Leann Benton, Bill Mann, Carlos Gallinger and Phil Benton standing by the Shaman's Cave. Photo by Don Taylor.

Directions: Exit I-15 at Baker and go south on KelBaker Road 13.0 miles, turn left and at 13.2 miles take the left fork for an additional 3.3 miles or 16.5 miles. Springs and petroglyphs are along wash system for approximately ½ mile. Shaman's Cave is on the left about two hundred yards from the end of the road. Look up and follow an ancient trail.

Location: S&C De Lorme, page 70, C-3

Coordinates: N35°13' .908', W115° 49'.138', elevation 2960' ± 160'

Vehicle: 4WD

Indian Ricegrass (*Oryzopsis Hymenoides*), also known as sand bunchgrass is common throughout the desert region. The seed was gathered and ground into flour.

17 MILE POINT
Petroglyph Site and Camp

Baker Area

Seventeen Mile Point got its name because it was almost halfway between Soda Springs and Marl Springs on the Old Mojave Road. It was thirty-four miles between these two springs. The Mojave Road came down around this lava flow and headed for Soda Lake. On the north side of this flow starting from the KelBaker Road are petroglyphs. Some of the panels are quite spectacular. The petroglyphs are scattered along the flow for almost one quarter of a mile. There are even some on boulders out in the wash along the flow. One good thing about this site is that you can drive on the pavement right up to the site and park in a small, open space and take a trail leading up to the petroglyphs along the face of the flow. It is a beautiful area and please don't touch the petroglyphs because they are an archeological treasure.

View of 17 Mile Point lava formation approaching from Baker on Kelbaker Road. Many petroglyphs can be found on the east side of this formation. Photo by Don Taylor.

Seventeen Mile Point campsite is the actual spot where the wagon trains camped. It is west of the petroglyph site but within view. This was a dry camp and a hard one especially for wagons headed east. From Soda Springs to Marl Springs it was uphill and sandy all of the way. The animals and the people suffered equally. The forage was almost non-existent. I am awed by what our pioneer ancestors endured to settle this country. Stop at this site and try to visualize the hustle and bustle of a wagon train of animals and people setting up camp, fixing meals, and caring for those sturdy animals. I love it!

Directions: From Baker south on Kelbaker Road 13.7 miles to where the lava flow reaches the road. There is a small place to park (five or six

Approaching 17 Mile Point from the Old Mojave Road just west of Kelbaker Road. Photo by Ron McKinley.

cars) and a trail leading to the petroglyphs. Campsite directions: Look to the northwest and you'll see a mesa approximately 3 miles away. Return to KelBaker road and drive toward Baker until you see a dirt road heading for the mesa. The campground is on the east side of the mesa near the north end.

Petroglyphs Location: S&C De Lorme, page 70, C-2

Coordinates for Petroglyphs: N35° 12' .327, W115° 52' .263', elevation 2214' ± 125'

Coordinates for Camp: N35° 13' 17", W115° 53' 30", elevation 1965' ± 125'

Vehicle: 2WD

The author and Don Putnam at the fire circle next to the actual 17 Mile Point. Photo by Ron McKinley.

Mormon Tea, Squaw Tea, Mexican Tea, Joint Fir (*Ephedra Spp.*). The twigs were boiled to make a beverage. Seeds were ground into a meal and prepared as a mush. Medicinally it was used for kidney and stomach ailments, colds and to purify the blood. There are 7 species of ephedra in the California deserts.

FOSSIL LAVA FALLS

Baker Area

This lava flow is starkly beautiful and looks so fresh you would think it could be hot. I would love to know how old it is. It is impressive! Some thousands of years ago a large sheet of lava was flowing slowly down a large wash. This wash is now called Aiken Wash after a cinder miner in the area. The flow went from one side of the wash to the other, then stopped. Now the drainage system goes over the top and forms an enormous waterfall. From below, it looks like a dam.

The mine to the north high on the cinder cone, is the Rainy Day Mine. They mined both red and black cinders, mostly for the concrete block industry.

This is beautiful country, especially in the spring. It is big horn sheep country, remote and pristine—so pack it in and pack it out.

Directions: To get to this site take the KelBaker Road off-ramp in Baker and turn south; at 16.5 miles turn north on the

Lava Falls across Aiken's Wash. Photos by Don Taylor.

Rainy Day Mine Road and drive alongside the lava flow. When you get to the end of the road, you hike and climb over the first small lava flow for about 150 yards and then you see the waterfall.

Location: S&C DeLorme, pg. 70, C-3

Coordinates: N35° 11' .086', W115° 49' .627', elevation: 3508' ± 125'

Vehicle: High clearance 2WD

The author on top of Lava Falls.

Aiken's Wash. You'll see a lot of this en-route to the Lava Falls. Below, petroglyphs around the Falls. Photos by Don Taylor

Milkweed (*Asclepias Spp.*). There are at least 12 species of milkweed in the California deserts. Indians ate flower buds, immature fruit pods and young shoots. The sap was used to make chewing gum. This plant is toxic if not prepared properly. Medicinally it is used to remove warts, treat cuts and burns, venereal disease and coughs. A solution from the seeds was used to draw poison from rattlesnake bites.

LAVA TUBE

Baker Area

When lava runs down the side of a volcano it is very heavy and seeks the lowest level. When it finds an old gully or wash it flows down like a molten river of liquid rock. As it flows the outside cools and hardens but the center continues to flow leaving a large, hollow empty tube. Inside the tube where the liquid lava pulled away from the hardened lava, all kinds of weird formations occur. Over the hundreds of years a few small places in the ceiling have opened up and fallen in, so there are rays of light shining down into the tube. This creates an out-of-this world, weird atmosphere. I really enjoy this tube.

The author and Gary Wilson at the entrance to the Lava Tube. All photos of this site by Ron McKinley

You must be careful as you go from room to room not to bump your head because the lava is very sharp. There has been some digging on the west end of the tube looking for a "river of gold". Be careful climbing down the steel ladder that leads into the tube. Look out for trolls!

Directions: Exit I-15 at Kelbaker Road to the south. At 12.6 road to left goes to Indian Springs. At 13.3 on left side is 17 Mile Point. At 13.6 the Old Government Road crosses the highway. At 13.7 the Old Mojave Road crosses the highway. At 16.2 you'll be abeam a cinder cone area on the left side. At 19.4 turn left onto Aiken Mine Road. At 20.9 the Old Mojave Road crosses at an angle. At 21 miles you'll pass an old corral on the left. At 23.8 you come to a fork and take the left fork. At 24 miles you come to another corral—bear left around this corral. At 24.3 park your vehicle. There's a rock cairn on the left side. To your left will be a cinder cone gully where the lava tube has completely collapsed. Walk over the small hill to your right and you'll see the entrance.
Location: S&C De Lorme, pg. 70, C-3
Coordinates: N35° 12' .958', W115° 45' .099', elevation 3560' ±
Vehicle: High Clearance 2WD

Author inside the Lava Tube. Note sunlight streaming through an opening above.

Hey! It's dark in here guys!

Top left and bottom right, the author in various parts of the Lava Tube.

A topside view of the Lava Tube.

LAVA ARCH

Baker Area

Lava Arch is a real unique structure. We think it was formed when a sheet of molten lava came down a hillside along a wash. It flowed over a soft spot such as a sand dune. Over hundreds and maybe thousands of years the soft material under the lava eroded away leaving an arch or giant bubble under the lava. The stream in the wash opened up the bubble and gave access to the Indians. The Indians evidently lived under the arch for many years and used the ceiling to paint many beautiful paintings or pictographs. They also had metatés in the large boulders where they could grind their mesquite beans and other seeds out of the weather. On each side of the arch and on the outside, they pecked many beautiful petroglyphs of every description. On the right side of the arch is the petroglyph of a large snake crawling over a rock. They used a small gas bubble in the rock as its eye.

This is a beautiful, precious, world class archeological site so please do not touch either the petroglyphs or the pictographs because they are very fragile. It is an easy one-half mile hike down the Aiken Wash to this site. If you look closely during the hike you will see petroglyphs on both sides of this wash. I hope you enjoy this site as much as I have. It is one of my favorites!

View of the Lava Arch when approaching from parking area. Photo by Ron McKinley.

Directions: Exit I-15 at Kelbaker Road to the south. At 12.6 road to left goes to Indian Springs. At 13.3 on left side is 17 Mile Point. At 13.6 the Old Government Road crosses the highway. At 13.7 the Old Mojave Road crosses the highway. At 16.2 you'll be abeam a cinder cone area on the left side. At 19.4 turn left onto Aiken Mine Road. At 20.9 the Old Mojave Road crosses at an angle. At 21 miles you'll pass an old corral on the left. At 23.8 you come to a fork and take the left fork. At 24 miles you come to another corral—take the right fork. At 24.8 bear left onto Aiken

Cinder Mine Road. When you pass through the mine area bear left. At 28.2 take sharp left onto Heritage Trail at the rock cairns on the left. At 28.9 park. Follow lava formations northwest until you see what looks like a cave—then cut across Aiken Wash to the cave. This is about a .6 mile walk.

Location: S&C De Lorme, page 70, C-3

Coordinates: N35° 14' .433', W115° 44' .345', elevation 3580' ±

Coordinates at Arch: N35° 14' .501', W115° 44' .836'.

Vehicle: High Clearance 2WD

Unusual red pictographs. Photo by Ron McKinley.

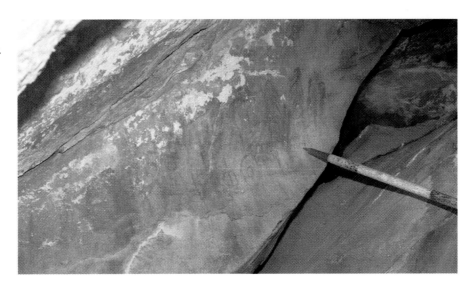

Members of the MRVM looking through the Arch from above. Photo by Phil Benton.

Left, a lava bomb held by the author. Right petroglyphs at the site. Photos by Don Taylor.

A volcanic bomb is a glob of molten lava that was blown into the air while liquid, then cooled and hardened while in the air. They are usually rounded or oblong and twisted at the ends because they twisted and tumbled while in the air. The bomb shown in my hands in the picture is a good example of such a volcanic bomb. What a sight this must have been to see. Mother Nature must have been on a temper tantrum to have caused this!

Author standing under the Arch. Photo by Ron McKinley.

LITTLE COW HOLE MOUNTAIN MILL SITES
Plus Old Well And Corrals

Baker Area

On the northeastern shore of Soda Lake and the side of Little Cow Hole Mountain are the ruins of two extensive mills. They were built at this location because gravity of the hillside could be used to move the ore through the mill. It was also close to much needed water to process the ore. In front of the mill site you can see the well and remains of the corrals with pens for the animals. The oldest mill site is the one closest to the lake and dates around the turn of the century. The other, and larger mill, is newer. It is rumored that the mills were built to process ore from the mines in the Old Dad Mountains to the southwest. The Mojave Trail passes nearby and is within eyesight. Numerous prospect holes are nearby. There are awesome views in all directions. A beautiful place to picnic. Or camp there and explore.

Ruins of the ore chute. Photo by Ron McKinley.

Directions: Exit I-15 to the south on Kelbaker Road at Baker. Between 6 and 8 miles look to your left and you can see the very prominent notch in the mountain, left of that is the Shaman's Eye and left of that is Squaw Tit—all prominent points used for navigation in the early days. At 12.3 miles turn right onto dirt road. At 13.1 you pass the actual 17 Mile Point and campsite. The old government road comes into the point from the left (east). At 13.5 continue on the old government road (Mojave Road) as it follows the contours of the mountains. At 15.1 you cross the Branigan Mine Road. The mine is to your left. The mountains on your left are the Old Dad Mountains. Ahead on the left are the Cowhole Mountains—on the right the Little Cowhole Mountains. At 17.5 you come to a crossroad with an old watering trough. Continue on the Mojave Road toward Soda Dry Lake. At 21.3 take right fork. At 22.2 you'll see the ruins of two old ore processing mills.

Location: S&C DeLorme, pg. 70, C-1.5

Coordinates: N35° 09' .798', W116° 01' .732', elevation: 735' ± 125'

Vehicle: High clearance 2WD

Concrete ruins of the mill-site. Photo by Ron McKinley.

View of the well and corral with Soda Dry Lake in the background.
Photo by Ron McKinley.

Photo of the mill in operation during the 1920s. Photo courtesy Dennis Casebier.

HOUSE IN THE SKY
and Lake View Mining Camp at Little Cow Hole Mountains

Baker Area

Several years ago, my friend, Joe Pizzatola, noticed a fairly large house in a little blind canyon near the top of Little Cow Hole Mountains. He was flying over the area in a helicopter to service communications equipment and just happened to look down and saw the house. He marked it on the map and later drove to it. He then called me and we both went in and explored it. I marvel at the amount of work needed to build a house at this location. It is obvious that this is a mine camp because there are signs of mining and ruins of a cable tramway nearby. The roof of the house has partially collapsed but the kitchen with the old ice box and homemade stove is still there.

Top, view of the valley below and Soda Dry Lake from the House in the Sky. Below, ruins of the house. All photos by Ron McKinley.

You can't see the house until you are almost on top of it. 4WD will take you to within two hundred yards of it. On the desert floor when you enter this canyon, there is an interesting natural arch on the east side of the canyon mouth. Enjoy, but please leave it as

you found it. I don't have any history on this house.

Nearby is the Lake View Mining Camp. This is a small mining camp in a relatively pristine state. The cans are all soldered and the glass is mostly purple. The trails between the mines and camp and down to the lake show a lot of wear. I have hiked these trails and get great enjoyment out of imagining how it was when people lived here. There appears to be a grave across the ravine east of the most northerly rock shelter ruins. I know nothing of the history of this camp and would appreciate hearing from anyone who knows about this camp.

The name Cow Hole comes from the ranchers in the area digging a hole for a well near the shores of Soda Lake and then digging a trench down to it so the cattle could walk down and drink. This way the ranchers could avoid the expense of a windmill. The water had to be fairly close to the surface. I have Dennis Casebier to thank for this information. I hope you enjoy this site as much as I did. Take your time and explore it thoroughly and enjoy!

Directions: Exit to the south onto Kelbaker Road from I-15 at Baker. Set odometer to zero. Between 6 and 8 miles look to your left and you can see the very prominent notch in the mountains. This notch was mentioned several times as a landmark in old journals of the pioneers. Left of that is Shaman's Eye and left of that is Squaw Tit. At 12.3 miles right onto dirt road. At 13.1 you arrive at the actual 17 Mile Point. The Old Government Road comes into the point from the left (east). There is a fire circle on the east side of the point where the wagons were circled and the men camped. Continue on the Mojave Road as it follows the contours of the mountains. At 15.1 you cross the Branigan Mine Road. The mine is to the left. The mountains on the left are the Old Dad Mountains. Ahead on the left are the Cowhole Mountains—on the right the Little Cowhole Mountains. At 17.5 you come to a crossroad with an old watering trough. Continue on the Mojave Road toward Soda Dry Lake. At 21.3 take right fork. At 22.2 you'll see the ruins of two old mills for processing gold ore. Backtrack the way you came approximately one mile and follow dirt road to the NE (4WD) The road forks several times—stay right. You'll have to hike the last 200 yards into the canyon. Thanks, Joe!

Coordinates: N35° 10' .530', W116° 00 .098'

Location: S&C DeLorme, pg. 70, C-1.5

Vehicle: High clearance 2WD except for last mile—4WD.

Directions for Lake View Mining Camp: Back track to the west about a half mile and look for indentations in the hillside where tents and other makeshift dwellings were set up.

Coordinates for Lake View Mining Camp: N35° 10' .347', W116° 00' .942', elevation 1191' ± 144'.

Photo of the house, circa 1930s, courtesy of Dennis Casebier.

IBEX SPRINGS
Ghost Town and Indian Village

Shoshone-Tecopa Area

Ibex Springs is one of those unknown gems of the desert. One day in the 1970's, while I was prospecting for talc, I came over a hill and there it was—a complete little ghost town! I marveled about its history as I walked among the buildings. There were rock shelters above the springs where the pre-1900 gold miners lived and then the main camp was built as a talc camp. There are ancient Indian trails converging on the springs. I followed these trails and discovered a large group of sleeping circles southeast of the main camp. Just south of the camp are the ruins of a stamp mill and a pre-1900, small smelter dating from the gold mining days. I always enjoy visiting Ibex Springs when in the area.

One of the mine operations buildings. All photos of this site by Phil Benton.

One day an old timer told me it was to be bulldozed. I went to the people at Death Valley Monument and worked out a deal where our museum group, The Mojave River Valley Museum, would monitor it photographically each year. The government would let our group adopt it and not destroy it. Please, please be careful with fire if you camp here.

Listen carefully for the rustle of the ghosts of all the people that have come and gone in the last one hundred years.

Directions: Exit I-15 at Baker. Proceed north on State Highway 127 approximately 39.3 miles. Turn left just past a communications relay tower, on a well traveled dirt road that was once paved. Keep right and at approximately 4.8 miles look left for a rock cairn. Walk out 50 yards and you will see the circles of a large Indian camp. Proceed down the road and at 5.3 miles you will be at the ghost town of Ibex.
Location: S&C De Lorme, page 43, B-5
Coordinates: N35° 46' .352', W116° 24' .584', elevation 1117'
Vehicle: 4WD

One of the mine entrances.

Author and others looking at the Indian sleeping circles just a few hundred yards east of the mining camp living area

Ruins of one of the mine buildings.

AMARGOSA BORAX WORKS

Shoshone-Tecopa Area

On Highway 127 between Old Spanish Gentry Road and the Furnace Creek Road are ruins of stone buildings on both sides of the road. These are the ruins of the Amargosa Borax Works.

The Amargosa Borax Works was established in 1883 to produce borax in the summer when it was too hot in Death Valley for the borax to crystallize in the tanks. The main and biggest deposits were in Death Valley. There was a spring near the borax works to furnish water for the operation so there could be a continuous production of borax. If you look closely, there are ruins and other signs of this operation.

The tops of the tanks can be seen sticking out of the ground. Behind the tanks is the loading ramp. The ruins of a large, stone company building are directly across Highway 127. This operation was set up by William Coleman with the help of Borax Smith. A great place to enjoy—take only pictures and leave nothing but footprints.

Ruins of old stone building. Photo by Don Taylor.

Directions: Exit I-15 at Baker and go north on SH127 to Old Spanish Gentry Road—approximately 44 miles, take right onto Furnace Creek Road for another 5 miles.
Location: S &C DeLorme, page 55, A-5 x 6.5
Coordinates: N35° 53' .286', W116° 15" .426', elevation 1318' ± 126'
Vehicle: 2WD

Spring and borax mill. Photo by author.

Susan Sorrels in front of the Shoshone Museum and Chamber of Commerce. While you're in the Shoshone area be sure to stop in and visit this interesting museum. Susan is a descendant of the legendary Charlie Brown and she and other family members own the town of Shoshone. Photo by Don Taylor.

Ruins of an old stone building. Photo by Don Taylor.

ZABRISKIE

*Shoshone-
Tecopa Area*

Zabriskie was a major town site on the old Tonapah and Tidewater Railroad. This was where most of the ore from Death Valley was loaded on the trains. It was also the source of the supplies badly needed by the miners. It boomed when the T&T came up out of the Amargosa Gorge in 1907, and slowly faded away as the mines closed down and later as roads were built and trucks and cars took over. The T&T Railroad was never a profitable venture because of the many washouts and lack of enough volume. Zabriskie was named after Christian B. Zabriskie, Secretary-Treasurer of the T&T and a chief executive in Borax Smith's empire. Nothing remains but slabs and rubble and acres of debris—cans and broken glass. You can still see the T&T rail-bed and where the loading docks were. The area

Author looking over the town dump of soldered cans. All photos of this site by Don Taylor.

Pilings left over from the mining operation.

is full of memories and if you look closely, it will tell you its story. What a great place to explore.

Directions: At the junction of Highway 127 and Furnace Creek Road, take a
dirt road northeast along a power line road and in about a mile you will dead end into the T&T railroad bed and Zabriskie.
Location: S&C DeLorme, page 55, A-6.
Coordinates: N35° 54'.137', W116°15' .314', elevation 1331' ± 221'
Vehicle: High clearance 2WD

Mesquite. Both Honey Mesquite (*Prosopis Julifera*) and Screwbean Mesquite (*Prosopis Pubescens*) were staples for the desert Indians. Every part of the mesquite was used—bean pods, blossoms, leaves, thorns, roots, trunk bark and sap and dead limbs were used for firewood. Nutritionally, mesquite beans compare to barley. Medicinally, it has been used as an eyewash and for sore throats, laryngitis and stomach inflammation.

MYSTERY CIRCLES
And Talc Loading Ramp

Shoshone-Tecopa Area

There is a long row of intriguing circles depressed in the desert and running parallel to Old Spanish Gentry Road. They are both spectacular and mysterious. You can tell that they are very old. Who made them and why? Some say they were made by Paleo man for religious or mystical reasons. Others think they were made by the Chinese prospecting for borax. The large wooden bins to the north were built to store talc hauled down from the mines high on the Ibex Mountains to the west. The large, eighteen wheeled highway trucks couldn't reach the mines, so small trucks, many of them four wheel

One of the many circles that extend for almost a mile. Below, author points out several of them. Photos by Ron McKinley.

drive, brought the talc down and drove up the ramp in back and dumped the talc into the bin. A big rig then came by and loaded the talc by gravity. This method was mainly used by the Eclipse Talc Mine until fairly recently. Look them over carefully because they tell a story about the difficulties of getting talc to market. Thanks to Susan Sorrells of the Shoshone Museum for showing me this amazing site.

Directions: Exit I-15 at Baker onto SH127 north. Approximately 44 miles down the road you'll reach the junction of SH127 and Old Spanish Gentry Road. The talc loading bins are within sight of this junction. The mystery circles are .1 mile farther east from the loading bins and about 100 yards south of Old

Spanish Gentry Road. They run parallel to the road.
Coordinates: N35° 52' .262', W116°16' .487', elevation 1078' ± 244'
Location: S&C De Lorme, page 55, B-6
Vehicle: 2WD

View of the Mystery Circles in the foreground with the talc loading ramp in the background across the highway. Photo by Ron McKinley.

Closer view of the talc loading ramp. Photo by Don Taylor.

INYO COUNTY HOT SPRINGS

Shoshone-Tecopa Area

Inyo County Hot Springs is on the east side of the road, in the middle of the small community of Tecopa Hot Springs. People come from round the world to bathe in this hot mineral water. It is reputed to alleviate the pain of arthritis, rheumatism, and other ailments. There's two sections—one for the ladies and one for the men as swim suits are not allowed. Showers and toilets are provided and a shower is required before entering the pool. There are two large, concrete pools for each gender— one hot and the other hotter. They range from about 100° to 108° and you are advised to stay in them no longer than five minutes. I delight in soaking in these

Outside view of the hot springs. Photo by Don Taylor.

two pools after a day of hiking in the beautiful and historic desert surrounding this area. Somehow your troubles seem to disappear. The baths are closed from 7:00 a.m. to noon on Monday and Friday for cleaning but are open at all other times, twenty-four hours a day. There is a large camping and trailer park across the street with very reasonable rates. Come and enjoy these pools as I have and let them enrich your life and best of all—they're free!

Directions: Exit I-15 at Baker onto SH127 north. At 44 ± miles turn right onto Old Spanish Gentry Road. Go to the intersection of Tecopa Hot Springs Trail and turn left (north). About 1 ½ miles on the right is the building that houses the hot springs.
Location: S&C De Lorme, page 55, B-7
Coordinates: N35° 52' .316', W116°13' .913', elevation 1394' ± 282'
Vehicle: 2WD

Inside the "hottest" pool on the men's side. Photo by Ron McKinley.

Another inside view of the men's pool. Photo by Ron McKinley.

Yucca Whipplei (*Our Lord's Candle*) Joshua Tree (*yucca brevifolia*), Mojave Yucca (*yucca schidigera*), and Spanish Bayonet (*yucca bacatta*) make up the four yuccas of the Mojave Desert. All were useful to the Native Americans but specific plants were preferred for certain uses. The flower stalk, flower and fruit were eaten. Leaves were used for sandals, baskets, rope, needle and thread and bowstrings. The root was used for soap and shampoo. Medicinally, yucca has been used for arthritic pain.

GRIMSHAW RIPARIAN AREA

Shoshone-Tecopa Area

The Grimshaw Riparian area is the last remnant of the old Ancient Lake Tecopa where mastodons and other extinct animals roamed. The Shoshone Museum is in the final stages of assembling and restoring a fairly complete mastodon found in the area. When finished, it will be put on public display. The Grimshaw Riparian area is a fantastic and exciting bird viewing area. At any one time, many different kinds of waterfowl can be seen feeding in

The riparian area covers many acres in the Tecopa area. Note the long-legged fishermen in the bottom photo. Both photos by Don Taylor.

this ancient lakebed. I have seen egrets, many kinds of ducks and Canadian geese feeding and resting here. Bring your binoculars and plenty of film.

Directions: Exit I-15 at Baker onto Highway 127 north. Proceed to Tecopa. Go north from Tecopa through Tecopa Hot Springs 1.0 miles and you will be at the Grimshaw Riparian area. It is on your left and is well marked.
Location: S&C De Lorme, page 55, B-7
Coordinates: N35° 53' .117', W116° 14' .074', elevation: 1301' ± 270'
Vehicle: 2WD

__Piñon Pine__ (pinus monophylla) provided the pine nuts (seeds from the pine cone). These were highly prized by many Indian tribes in the SW. The nuts are nutritious and high in calories—about 2880 calories per pound. The needles are a good source of vitamin C and make a nice tea that has a mild diuretic and expectorant function. Pitch from the tree was used as a "band-aid", glue and water-proofing agent.

DUBLIN CITY AND SHOSHONE CEMETERY

Shoshone-Tecopa Area

Dublin City is a unique area that has a rather hard tufa cap on top with soft material underneath. The miners would pick and dig out rooms under the cap that faced a wash or drainage system. There is such an area just south and west of Shoshone. The miners that initially dug the first rooms were Irish, reportedly from Dublin, hence the name "Dublin City". The rooms were warm in the winter and cool in the summer. They even drilled holes through the tufa cap for the smoke to escape. As the years went by, the rooms became bigger and more elaborate. They began to be connected underground. After the

Dublin City miner's homes above and part of the Shoshone cemetery below right. Photos by Don Taylor.

automobile came into use, one miner even was said to dig out a garage. After World War II, an undesirable element moved in and controlled the area for many years. They are gone now and it is fun to explore and imagine how it would be to live in the "underground" city.

The Shoshone Cemetery is on the north bank and a little east of Dublin City. It is nostalgic to walk among the graves and try to visualize how life was in the old days. Let these hardly pioneers rest in peace. I have a great respect for them.

Directions: Exit I-15 at Baker and proceed north to Shoshone. Dublin City is just south of Shoshone and .1 or .2 miles west of Highway 127. The rooms carved under the tufa is called Dublin City. The cemetery is between Dublin City and Shoshone on the north bank of the drainage system.
Location: S&C De Lorme, page 55, A-6
Coordinates: N35° 58' .409', W116°16' .381', elevation 623' ± 190 feet
Vehicle: 2WD

MARTA BECKET'S OPERA HOUSE
At Death Valley Junction

Shoshone-Tecopa Area

Marta Becket is one of those phenomenal persons that one only meets once or twice in a lifetime. I have led many tours through the years to her show and the people have come away thrilled every time. She is a talented artist and a good opera performer. Viewing her murals is worth the admission price alone. Be sure to ask to see some of the rooms in the adjoining Death Valley Junction Hotel. As of May, 1999, she is still giving regular performances. You must see one of her performances. She is one of the great personalities of the Death Valley region. Call 760-852-4441 for reservations or more information. I guarantee you won't be sorry.

View of the opera house at the junction of highways. All photos on this page by Ron McKinley

Directions: The Amargosa Opera House is at Death Valley Junction near the intersection of Routes 127 and 190. Exit I-15 at Baker and stay on SH127 to Death Valley Junction. It is well marked.
Location: S&C De Lorme, page 43, B-5
Coordinates: N36° 18' 08", W116° 13' 27", elevation 2040' ± 180'
Vehicle: 2WD

Painted scenes in some of the bedrooms at the motel.

Videocaptures of Marta Becket's opera by
"Dave of the Dez" Williamson

Chia (*salvia columbariae*). Seed was eaten raw
or ground into flour for mush or cakes and was
also used to make a beverage. The nutritional
value was sufficient to keep a person going on a
forced march for 24 hours on just one teaspoon.
Seed was also used to remove material from the
eye and today is used as "Chia Pets."

CHIEF TECOPA'S HOUSE
and Castles in the Clay

Shoshone-Tecopa Area

A short distance from Shoshone just after you cross the Amargosa River is a clay point or cliff on your left. At the base of this clay cliff are several large Athol trees. Behind these trees, carved into the bank, is a large, underground home. When I was first shown this home by Celeste Gilliam many years ago, it was filled with crude, but functional furniture. She told me that this was

Above, outside view of the Chief's house. Below, inside views. Photos by Don Taylor.

the home of Chief Tecopa. There is some dispute about the inhabitant, but whoever carved it out made a most interesting place to live. It is cool in the summer and warm in the winter.

The canyon behind it also contains some underground dwellings. It is called *Castles in the Clay* because of the strange clay formations there. There is a beautiful hike along this historic area of the Amargosa River. In the spring it is loaded with flowers and birds. The area is posted "no camping" but owner Susan Sorrells assured me that camping here is okay. Her office is next to the post office in Shoshone. Be sure to pack it in and pack it out.

Directions: From the intersection of Highway 127 and Highway 178 near Shoshone, take Hwy 178 and the home will be behind some trees on your left. Castles in the Clay is in a canyon behind the trees.
Location: S&C De Lorme, page 55, A-6.5
Coordinates: N35° 58' .322', W116° 15' .55", elevation: 1519' ± 213'
Vehicle: 2WD

Looking out from the inside of the Chief's house.

Castles in the Clay. Photo by Don Taylor.

Creosote Bush, Chaparral, Greasewood (*larrea tridentata*), the most dominant shrub of the high and low deserts. Although not edible, creosote bush has many medicinal uses for colds, chest infections and congestion, joint pain and poultices. Researchers are looking at this plant for other uses such as a vegetable oil preservative and herbicide.

PERLITE COMET

Shoshone-Tecopa Area

Years ago, while traveling east on Highway 178 from Shoshone, I was startled to see in a highway cut, a large, shiny, jet black seam or streak of rock. It was spectacular and at first I thought it was coal or maybe perlite. I stopped, picked up some pieces, and put them in the campfire. They didn't burn as coal does or pop as perlite does. The streak shines or sparkles depending on how the sun is shining on it. In almost fifty years of mining and prospecting, I have never seen anything like this. I have heard it called black glass but it is not obsidian. Scientists haven't been able to classify it but say it's probably in the perlite family although there is no consensus on this. What ever it is, it is very unusual. It was formed by some cataclysmic explosion many millions of years ago. I am glad I wasn't around when it was formed! Geology teachers bring their classes here to study this wonder. I named it the Perlite Comet.

Directions: From the intersection of Highway 127 and 178 in Shoshone go 3.8 miles on Highway 178 and the Perlite Comet will be in a cut on the left side of the highway.
Location: S&C DeLorme, page 55, A-6.5
Coordinates: N35° 59' .801', W116°13' .131', elevation 2358' ± 186'
Vehicle: 2WD

Perlite Comet from the highway. Don Taylor poses in the picture to the right to give perspective to the view. Top photo by Don Taylor, below right by Phil Benton.

TWELVE MILE SPRING
Mortar Site, Roasting Pits and Purification Site

Shoshone-Tecopa Area

Twelve Mile Spring is one of those fantastic sights for which the Mojave Desert is famous. It is still used today as a purification site by a tribe of Indians from Nevada. They gather together under a hut made of cottonwood limbs and pvc pipe, covered with plastic, and drop hot rocks into the water, thus making steam. This makes them sweat and they call it purification. This is a large riparian area with springs cropping out from under a large tufa ledge or cap. Between the main spring area and some smaller springs to the south, there is a mortar area in the tufa cap. A mortar is a round hole in a large rock where Indians pounded seeds or beans into a powder. The more use the mortar gets the deeper it gets which make them more common in the foothills or mountains where acorns and pinion nuts are plentiful. Mortars are rare in the desert and these mortars are some of the deepest I have ever seen. I marvel on how they could

grind their meal in such deep holes. Away from the ancient mortars to the east are a series of roasting pits. It is obvious that this site has been used for a very long time. Take nothing but pictures, leave nothing but footprints.

Directions: From the intersection of Highway 127 and Highway 178 in Shoshone, go east for 5.4 miles on Highway 178 and turn off on the Chicago Valley Road and at 6.1 miles continue on straight along a power-line road. Go past a well, onto a playa, and stay on

View of the spring as you approach. All photos of this site by Don Taylor.

the well-traveled road. (Note: you are crossing private property to get to the spring so please respect the land owner's property and facilities.) Stay to the left across the playa to a group of trees on the north east side of the playa and at 8.6 miles you will be at the springs. Mortars are 150 to 200 yards from the springs at 100° compass heading. Roasting pits are .4 miles at 052° degrees from the springs. A trace road goes by the pits. Follow low creek bed.
Location: S&C DeLorme, page 43, D-7
Coordinates: N36° 01' .308', W116° 09' .248', elevation: 2141' ± 251'
Vehicle: 4WD

Author points out mortars in the sandstone near the spring.

52

Indian purification frame just a few yards from the spring.

Cactus in bloom near the spring. Photo by Mike McCain.

TRILOBITE SITE

Shoshone-Tecopa Area

High on the side of the Resting Springs Range of Mountains, at the end of a short dirt road, is a deposit of ancient shale. This shale was deposited millions of years ago as mud and each season washed in another layer. The layers built up each year somewhat like rings in a tree and became very hard after being compressed in the earth's crust. In these layers lived a primitive crab-like creature much like our present day horseshoe crab. These impressions and fossils are eagerly sought after. They come from the Paleozoic Era and can be found by splitting the layers. You can see where people split and dug the shale. I asked our famous Lake Manley fisherman, Don Putnam, if this is where he got his bait! This is a beautiful, historic area to camp in and explore. Remember—pack it in and pack it out!

Myrtie Keddy Putnam digs for trilobites. Photo by Don Putnam.

Directions: Exit I-15 at Baker and turn north on SH127. At approximately 44 miles turn right onto Old Spanish Gentry Road and continue another 4 miles to the intersection of the Old Spanish Trail Road and Furnace Creek Road east of the town of Tecopa. Re-set odometer to zero. Proceed northerly on the old Spanish Trail Road 8.7 miles and turn left on a well traveled dirt road. Road ends at the diggings in about .2 miles.

Location: S&C DeLorme, page 56, A-1

Coordinates: N35° 53' .422', W116° 04' .371', elevation 2460' ± 222'

Vehicle: 2WD except for the last ½ mile

Photograph of a fossilized trilobite courtesy of the National Archives.

Since these critters are very faint and hard to photograph here's a line drawing of one.

EMIGRANT PASS
Mule Trail & Wagon Road

Shoshone-Tecopa Area

From the top of Emigrant Pass you have a beautiful view north and beyond the Chicago Valley. You can see the wagon road wandering to Stump Springs and on to the horizon. To the south you get an awesome view of the Armagosa River Valley and the Grimshaw Lake plus mountain range after mountain range. I wonder what the weary pioneers said when they topped the pass and saw what laid before them. I don't think they saw the beauty in it that I do.

View of Emigrant Pass from the top showing the wagon road coming over the top. Photos by the author.

Both the wagon road and mule trail are still very much in evidence. There is a good view of the mule trail going down on the west side of the pass. A white monument marks where it goes over the top. The wagon road goes over the top and south into a wash, then climbs out on top of the west side and travels parallel to the wash for a long way. This is a well preserved section and you can see in many places where the iron rims hit the rocks. Please do not take motorized vehicles on any section of this wagon road. The next stop was Resting

Above, long view of the mule trail over the pass. Photo by the author.

Springs where the pioneers would rest and repair their wagons and equipment. Walk on these roads and trails and try to visualize the hundreds and hundreds of our ancestors struggling over the desert to a new and hopefully better life.

Directions: From I-15 at Baker exit north on Highway 127 and go to Tecopa. Start from the intersection of the Old Spanish Trail Road and Furnace Creek Road east of the town of Tecopa. Proceed northerly on the old Spanish Trail Road for 7.6 miles and walk across the wash approximately 100 yards and the wagon road will be on top of the west bank. Proceed 9.6 miles to dirt road to the left and at 9.8 miles you will be on top of Immigrant Pass. Both the mule trail and wagon road are very visible. A white monument marks where the mule trail goes over the pass.
Location: S&C De Lorme, page 43, D-7
Coordinates: Mule Train, N35° 53' 13", W116° 03' 43.5", elevation 3264' ± 275'
Wagon Road: N35° 53' .371', W116° 05' .426', elevation 1798'
Vehicle: 2WD

Dramatic view of the wagon road.
Photo by Gina Robison.

NOONDAY MINE TOWN SITE

Shoshone-Tecopa Area

The ruins on each side of Furnace Creek Road are what is left of the ghost town of Noonday. When the Tonapah and Tidewater Railroad came up out of the Amargosa Gorge in 1907, the town known as Old Tecopa moved west to its present location to be on the railroad at the top of the gorge. In 1909, construction started on the Tecopa Railroad to connect the Noonday and Gunsite Mines with the main line of the Tonapah and Tidewater at new Tecopa. This line was finished in 1910, and furnished cheap transportation for the ore of the Tecopa Mines, consisting of the Gunsite-Noonday, War Eagle, and other mines of the area. The principal mineral produced was lead used for lead based paint, some silver, and some gold. The town of Noonday grew up at its present location because of its closeness to the mines and the railroad. After a shaky start, a man named Dr. Lincoln Godshall, noted chemist and mining engineer, took control and turned it into the greatest producing mine of the Death Valley area. For sixteen years, he made daily shipments of ore of 75 to 200 tons and when he was finally forced to shut down in 1928, he had shipped almost 150,000 tons of ore. His grandson and wife, Dr. and Mrs. Harry Godshall, own the beautiful Resting Springs Ranch and graciously let the MRVM use it as a base camp. They are delightful people and we have become close friends. This entire historic area is a great place to explore but remember what Shortfuse says about mines: stay out and stay alive!

Directions: Start from intersection of the Old Spanish Trail Road and Furnace Creek Road east of the town of Tecopa. Proceed east on Furnace Creek Road for 6.7 miles and the ruins of the ghost town of Noonday will be on both sides of the road.
Location: S&C DeLorme, Page 56, B-1
Coordinates: N35° 48' .614', W116° 06' .231', elevation 2165' ± 174'
Vehicle:
2WD

View of ruins from near the highway looking toward the mines in the hills beyond. All photos of this site by Ron McKinley.

Left, a home-made but still functional weather vane among the ruins. Below, Don Putnam points to the mines in the surrounding hills.

Old Engine at Tecopa, Calif.

Left a locomotive that once served the Noonday Mine. Below, one of the Noonday Mines in operation. Photos from postcards at the Shoshone Museum.

Noonday Mine

58

OLD TECOPA

Shoshone-Tecopa Area

Old Tecopa began in the 1870's as a supply center for area mines. It also contained a large mill and furnace for processing the local ore. It was centrally located between the Tecopa Mines on the north and the Alexander Mines on the south. There are extensive ruins in the area. You can prowl around the ruins of the old mill and see the slag left over from Jonas Osborne's smelter that was completed in

Above, the town of Old Tecopa was in this little valley across the road from the mill but not much is left now. Below, on the hill east of the town and across the road is the cemetery. Photo by the author.

1878. It is in the bottom of the canyon below the rest of the ruins. There is a small, quaint cemetery overlooking Tecopa on the end of a point before you turn off Furnace Creek Road. Look for my cairn. Please let these hardy pioneers rest in peace.

Tecopa is the Indian name for wildcat or bobcat. Tecopa flourished but died a sudden death when the Tonapah and Tidewater Railroad emerged from the Amargosa Gorge in 1907 and the town moved to its present location. There was some recent activity in the area due to talc mining and there were attempts to rework some of the old mine dumps.

Take nothing but pictures and leave nothing but footprints. This is a very historic area. Close your eyes and try to visualize all the activity that went on here many years ago.

Directions: Exit I-15 at Baker and turn north on SH127. At approximately 44 miles turn right onto Old Spanish Gentry Road and continue another 4 miles to the intersection of the Old Spanish Trail Road and

Photo of cemetery by Gina Robison.

Furnace Creek Road east of the town of Tecopa. Re-set odometer to zero. The ruins of the mill will be at 7.6 miles on Furnace Creek Road. Old Tecopa is right across the street and continues down the canyon.

Cemetery Directions: At 7.3 miles on the left or east side of the road on top of the ridge.

Location: S&C DeLorme, page 56, B-1

Mill Coordinates: N35° 47' .980', W116° 05' .960', elevation 2130' ± 136'

Cemetery Coordinates: N35° 48' .116', W116° 05' .981', elevation: 2642' ± 168'

Vehicle: 2WD

Above, view of the mill from the highway. Below, different views of the mill. All photos by Ron McKinley.

GRAND CANYON OF THE TECOPA

Shoshone-Tecopa

The Grand Canyon of the Tecopa is one of those breathtaking surprises that you happen on a few times in your lifetime. It is an undiscovered gem of the desert. The views are awesome and change hourly, especially in the afternoon. If you look carefully, you will be surprised to see the ruins of a ranch house in the bottom of this deep canyon. This is where Lois Clark, the editor of the Baker Valley News, lived as a child. Her father worked in the nearby talc mines. There is a trail that leads down the steep canyon walls to the ranch. It is not for the faint hearted. I have built a cairn at the top. Hold on to your kids while exploring this area as the walls are straight up and down in places and are hundreds of feet high.

Left looking south into the canyon. Above, looking east into the canyon. All photos on this page by Ron McKinley.

This is an awesome place to visit and explore.

Directions: Start at the intersection of the Old Spanish Trail Road and the Furnace Creek Road, just east of the town of Tecopa. Proceed east on Furnace Creek Road, past the China Ranch turnoff sign, to a pole line road 4.2 miles. Turn right and at .6 miles you will be at the overlook.
Location: S&C DeLorme, page 55 B-7
Coordinates: N35° 48' .461', W116° 08' .760', Elevation: 1902' ± 53'
Vehicle: 2WD

*Note trail descending into the canyon.
Imagine Lois Clark using this trail as a
child--even at night! Photo by Ron
McKinley.*

View looking west into the canyon.

62

Before and after views of the old ranch house in the bottom of the canyon. Original photo above, courtesy of Lois Clark who lived there as a child. Current photos by Ron McKinley.

Indian trail near the canyon. Photo by Phil Benton.

En-route to the Grand Canyon of the Tecopa on Furnace Creek Road, look for the "Middle-of-the-road" Thunderbird .4 mile after passing China Ranch Road. An artist from Mexico, Escubio Villa, was working with the crew that paved the road and used left-over asphalt to create this scene. He did other scenes on the roads in this area so look for them as you travel through. Photo by Ron McKinley.

CHINA RANCH

Shoshone-Tecopa Area

China Ranch is one of those splendid surprises in life. You drive over the drab desert and down a nondescript canyon and suddenly a beautiful, hidden oasis appears in front of you.

For a moment you think: "Am I transported to the Sahara Desert or am I in the middle of a mirage?" There are tall date palms next to green fields of alfalfa with a little stream gurgling down the middle. The first time I visited years ago, the fields were full of three kinds of melons and a man named Brian Brown was tending a large number of bee hives. I admire Brian and his wife, Bonnie. They have worked hard transforming China Ranch into a paying proposition, raising a family and pouring every 18,000 bricks for a beautiful adobe home. Take your time here and read the signs that tell the history of China Ranch. Listen to Brian and Bonnie explain the sex life of a date palm. It is fascinating. Whatever you do, make certain you have one of their delicious date shakes! Tell them Shortfuse sent you.

Right, the author standing in front of the welcome sign. Photo by Don Taylor. Below, standing in front of the gift shop. Photo by Ron McKinley.

Directions: From I-15 exit on Highway 127 north. At Tecopa take Old Spanish Trail Road east and follow the large China Ranch signs.
Location: S&C De Lorme, page 55, B-7
Coordinates: N35° 48' .018', W116° 11' .680', elevation: 1395' ± 249'
Vehicle: 2WD

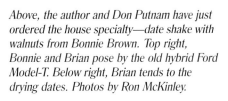

Above, the author and Don Putnam have just ordered the house specialty—date shake with walnuts from Bonnie Brown. Top right, Bonnie and Brian pose by the old hybrid Ford Model-T. Below right, Brian tends to the drying dates. Photos by Ron McKinley.

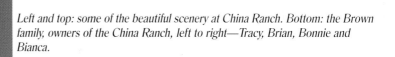

Left and top: some of the beautiful scenery at China Ranch. Bottom: the Brown family, owners of the China Ranch, left to right—Tracy, Brian, Bonnie and Bianca.

STAGE COACH STATION

Shoshone-Tecopa Area

Take a short hike down a beautiful canyon below historic China Ranch and you come to a quaint building. This lovely building is built from hand carved tufa blocks and over the door is carved the date 1903. I have been told that this building was a saloon and a way station or a stage station on the wagon road. Whatever it was, it is in need of restoration because a recent earthquake badly damaged it. Years ago, I led a museum field trip here and a woman found an 1872 Indian Head penny in the doorway of this quaint, historic building.

Directions: Park car at China Ranch Gift Shop and hike an easy, interesting trail approximately ½ mile along Willow Springs Wash.
Location: S&C DeLorme, page 55, B-7
Coordinates: N35° 47' .635', W116° 11' .990', elevation 1619' ± 254'
Vehicle: 2WD

Right, Don Putnam and Phil Benton checking out the old stage coach station. Below, another view of the ruins. Photos by Don Taylor.

ACME

Shoshone-Tecopa Area

Park car at China Ranch gift shop and hike on an easy, interesting and historic trail approximately 3/4 mile along Willow Springs Wash to the Indian village site.

On the top of a bluff overlooking the confluence of the Amargosa Gorge and the Willow Springs Canyon is a large concentration of sleeping circles. It also overlooks the site of Acme. Acme was a site on the

This scene is the Acme railroad siding in China Ranch. Photo by Don Taylor.

Tonapah and Tidewater Railroad where they loaded gypsum and talc on the railroad cars. It was also where a short, steep branch of the railroad went to China Ranch to load gypsum directly from the mine. One day while loading gypsum the train got away from the crew, roared down the canyon, and derailed near Acme killing the engineer. You can see the old gypsum mines on both sides of the canyon just above China Ranch.

As you stand on the point of the bluff among the sleeping circles overlooking Acme, look around you. You are not only standing in a very historic area, but you are also in a very spectacular and beautiful scenic area as well. The birds and flowers are beautiful in season in this riparian area. Pack it in and pack it out.

Ruins of an old ore loading chute. Photo by Don Taylor.

Directions: Park car at China Ranch gift shop and hike on an easy, interesting and historic trail approximately ¾ mile along Willow Springs Wash.
Location: S&C DeLorme, page 55, B-7
Coordinates: N35° 47' .414', W116°12' .045', elevation 1295' ± 208 feet
Vehicle: 2WD

Ruins of another ore loading chute. Photo by Don Taylor.

Don Putnam and the author standing among Indian sleeping circles.

AMARGOSA GORGE

Shoshone-Tecopa Area

Amargosa Gorge adjoins the town of Tecopa on the west and south. The gorge is one of the true gems of the Mojave Desert. It is a beautiful hike to go down the gorge on the old Tonapah & Tidewater Railroad rail bed to Acme and then up Willow Wash to China Ranch. It is about a five mile hike through some of the most beautiful and spectacular desert scenery that exists. You will pass riparian areas filled with many kinds of birds and pass by massive rock formations of every hue and color. You will pass a waterfall and ruins of the old T&T. If you look on top of the ridges, you will see evidence of where human beings lived and camped centuries ago.

The Amargosa Gorge is a favorite place and I always get a thrill when I hike down or up it. Take my advice, see it and enjoy it like I have. Be prepared: bring plenty of water and a camera with lots of film. Also, wear good hiking shoes.

Directions: In Tecopa, turn south on the dirt road that goes by the post office and church and stay on the only road that runs alongside the gorge. The roads ends in about ½ mile.
Location: S&C De Lorme, page 55, B-6
Coordinates: N35° 50' 42", W116°13' 27", elevation: 1185 ± 235
Vehicle: 2WD

Above, un-identified hikers in Amargosa Gorge. Below, a sweeping view of the gorge. Photos by Rose Foster-Villegas.

HEPATITIS SPRINGS

Shoshone-Tecopa Area

Hepatitis Springs was named by some unknown character because it was completely open and unregulated. In the old days when I first visited it, it was pretty trashy, but when I last visited it in October, 1999, it was immaculate. There is a small, concrete tank with warm water running through it. The springs are on the side of a small hill and has a beautiful view. I love to bathe in a place such as this that is completely free and unregulated. The people that I have met here are friendly and understanding. If nudity offends you, stay away. The swim suit companies are not going to do well here. It's a nice spot to camp and costs nothing. Be sure to pack it in and pack it out. Let's try to keep this spot free and unregulated.

Directions: Exit I-15 at Baker and proceed north to Tecopa. Go east from Tecopa on old Spanish Trail for 1.3 miles and turn sharp left and at 3.1 miles you will be at the hot springs. Hot springs are on the hill to your left. Continue on the road 1.2 miles and you come out on the Tecopa Hot Springs road north of the town by the Grimshaw riparian area.

Location: S&C De Lorme, page 55, B-7
Coordinates: N35° 52' .5', W116°13' .109', elevation 1375' ± 220'
Vehicle: 4WD

Famous male center-fold model, Phil Benton, tests the waters in Hepatitis Springs.

HALLORAN SPRINGS

Turquoise Mountain Area

Halloran Springs is an important historical and archaeological site. It's located at an intersection of old trails and wagon roads and an important water source to this day. It's reportedly named after a cavalry officer stationed at Camp Cady. A welcome site by many a thirsty, weary, overland traveler. It is still being used as an important watering site for cattle and wildlife and you will often see burros and cattle watering there. It is a beautiful site in the spring when the wildflowers are blooming but rather bleak and barren the balance of the year.

On a lava flow on each side of a large wash there is a scattering of petroglyphs. These low ridges parallel and are very close to I-15. There are several nice panels and a deeply carved "T. C.". I wonder who the T.C. is? It seems to have some age. This site is alongside one of the old highway 91 road beds. If these ridges could talk, what a story they could tell! Directions for the petroglyphs: Exit I-15 at Halloran Springs to the north. At .1 mile turn right onto dirt road (old Highway 91) go half a mile to lava rock formations on right side. Coordinates for petroglyphs: N35° 22' .708', W116° 53' .050', elevation 3046' ± 362'Enjoy!

Note: From time to time signs appear just beyond Halloran Springs that warn that the "road is private and no trespassing." The road and the land is public so just ignore these signs if you see them.

A wild burro approaches the watering tank at Halloran Springs. Photo by Don Taylor.

Directions: Exit I-15 at Halloran Springs off-ramp and cross freeway northbound. At .7 miles on the right is Halloran Springs.
Location: S&C DeLorme, p. 70, A-5, 2.5
Coordinates: N35° 22' .976', W115° 53' .050', elevation 2768' ± 153'
Vehicle: 2WD

Wild burros abound around Halloran Springs. Photo by Ron McKinley.

This is the spring at Halloran. Someone has covered it to slow evaporation and added a pipe to pipe water to watering tanks nearby. Photo by Ron McKinley.

HALLORAN SPRINGS RUINS

Turquoise Mountain Area

These ruins are on the old historic Arrowhead Highway that became Highway 91 and are rumored to be the first Halloran Springs store and gas station. It is on the crossroads where several roads came together at Halloran Springs. In those days the trails or wagon roads went from waterhole to waterhole. These waterholes or springs were very important and many times were lifesavers. It was a very active mining area so it would make sense that this would be a supply center. I don't know much about these ruins and would appreciate any information that one might have. There is also some mining activity back of the ruins. It is a great place to explore and enjoy. Try visualizing living out here so many years ago. Think how these people survived! It is fun!

Directions: Exit I-15 at Halloran Springs off-ramp, then go across freeway northbound to Halloran Springs .7 miles on the right; at fork in the road bear left 1.0 mile and ruins are 1.3 miles on your left.
Location: S&C De Lorme, page 70, A-2
Coordinates: N35° 23' .234', W115° 54' .136', elevation 2900' ± 171'
Vehicle: 2WD

Not much is left of the settlement—only a few rusty cans. Photo by Don Taylor.

Ruins of the first store and gas station. Photo by Ron McKinley.

WANDER MINE

Turquoise Mountain Area

The Wander Mine is in a highly mineralized area that has been mined off and on for over a hundred years. I put it as a site to visit because it is in a very historic area and is both mysterious and interesting. What is the story of the well-made cross at the top of the diggings? Did some unfortunate miner lose his life here? The mine shows evidence of being worked before the turn of the century—during the depression and as late as 1950. The gold is in a quartz vein that wanders down the side of a hill, thus its name. There are numerous shafts and "glory holes" in the area, so remember what Shortfuse says about climbing down old mine shafts. Don't! There are miner's rock shelters, foundations and old dumps in the area. The mine is high on the foothills of the Turquoise Mountains with beautiful views in all directions. A great place to explore.

Note: From time to time signs appear just beyond Halloran Springs that warn that the road

is "private and no trespassing." The road and the land is public so just ignore these signs if you see them.

Directions: Exit I-15 at Halloran off-ramp, cross the freeway headed north. At .7 mile, the springs will be on your right. There is a fork at 1.0 miles and bear left. There will be ruins at 1.3 miles. At 1.7 miles you will come to a tee; go left for about 100 yards and turn right on a well traveled dirt road. At 2.3 miles, keep to the right. At 3.7 miles you are at the town site of Halloran. Continue on and at 4.1 miles keep right. At 4.75 you will pass an old auto club sign post. At 5.2 miles you will be at the Wander Mine. Look to the left for a large, white cross and the mine wanders down a rock ridge for about ¼ mile.
Location: S&C DeLorme, page 70, A-2
Coordinates: N35° 24' 10", W115° 57' 47", elevation 3275' ± 320'
Vehicle: High Clearance 2WD

Left, author holding part of an old explosives box next to the powder magazine. Above, the town dump of rusty tin cans. Photos by Don Taylor.

GUZZLER

Turquoise Mountain Baker Area

A guzzler is an installation designed to collect and store rainwater for wildlife. In this case, it is a concrete apron on a slope that collects and channels the water into an underground storage area for birds and other small animals. It is fenced to keep burros and other large animals out and has a small opening to allow only small critters in. In this case, a private wildlife organization, San Pedro Chapter of the Izak Walton League, is maintaining it. It really helps small wildlife to get through drought conditions. These people should be commended for their efforts. These guzzlers are not usually so accessible and are a treat to visit.

Directions: Exit I-15 at Halloran Springs off-ramp and head north. At .7 miles Halloran Springs is on your right. At 1.0 mile bear left. At 1.3 miles you'll pass the ruins on the left. At 1.7 miles you come to a tee, go left and 100 yards later turn right. At 2.3 miles you come to a fork, keep right. At 3.7 miles you come to the old townsite of Halloran on the right (noth-

The Guzzler water collection chute and tank that catches rainfall and preserves it for small wildlife in the area. Two views, top and bottom right. Photos by Ron McKinley.

ing left but old cans between two large Joshua trees. At 4.1 keep right. At 4.75 you will go past an old Auto Club sign-post, keep right. At 5.2 miles you will be at the Wander Mine. Take right fork at mine. At 6.3 take the left fork and look immediately for the guzzler on the right. At 6.4 you're there.

Location: S&C DeLorme, pg 70, A-2
Coordinates: N35° 25' .166', W115° 57' .809', elevation 2309' ± 288'
Vehicle: 4WD

LEAVE US ALONE

INDIAN TURQUOISE MINE

Turquoise Mountain Area

The Indian Turquoise Mine, also known as the Toltec Mine, is an awesome hole in the ground high on the side of the Turquoise Mountains. The view from the mine is breath-taking. The mine is one large "glory hole" with numerous tunnels following small seams of turquoise. There has been a lot of beautiful turquoise taken out of here but unfortunately, it seems to be very hard to find now. We looked and were rewarded with a few small chips. The Indians prized this turquoise and used quartz tools to pry it out. Some of these tools have been found. It is rumored that the early Spanish also mined these gems here. This particular mine produced a dark, robin-egg-blue stone that was very prized.

The out-croppings are very beautiful. Some of these veins are quartz that also carry a trace of gold so you can see small prospect holes over a large area of these mountains. There are also other turquoise sites. The last 1.2 miles to the Toltec is for the serious, experienced four-wheel driver only! My wife kept her eyes closed but enjoyed the view once we arrived. Be careful and enjoy it. This is an awesome spot.

Approach view of the mine. All photos of this site by Ron McKinley.

Directions: Exit I-15 at Halloran Springs and go north. (This is tough to find so pay attention!) Halloran Springs is on the right at .7 mile. At 1.0 mile take the left fork. Ruins are at 1.3 on the left. At 1.7 miles you'll come to a tee in the road, go left. 100 yards later turn right. At 2.3 you come to a fork, keep right. At 3.7 on the right is the old Halloran townsite. At 4.75 you go past an old Auto Club sign post, keep right. At 5.2 miles you come to the Wander Mine. Take right fork at mine and at 6.3 miles take the left fork and look for the guzzler on the right at 6.4 miles. At 6.5 miles bear left and at 7.1 miles turn right at rock cairn. Now comes the serious 4WD part. Follow road/trail for 1.2 miles and at 8.3 you're there.
Location: S&C DeLorme, pg 70, A-2
Coordinates: N35° 25' 48", W115° 57' 29", Elevation 3756 ± 342'
Vehicle: 4WD

Looking down into the mine.

Another view of the mine.

Don and Myrtie Putnam navigate the gnarly road to the mine.

CARTOONS BY ROCKY

TURQUOISE PEAK COMMUNICATIONS CENTER

Turquoise Mountain Area

This was a super secret installation built at the height of the Cold War in the 1960's. It was built as part of a system so our government could communicate with the armed forces worldwide during a nuclear war and was built to withstand an atomic blast and still function. It is of heavy reinforced concrete and extends, I understand, three or four stories down into the mountain in solid rock. At the height of its operations, there were fifty or sixty men operating it twenty-four hours a day. It is vacant now with some automatic equipment still functioning. The road is open and paved to the top. There is a small turn-around area with an awe-

Part of the sweeping view from the peak. All photos of this site by Ron McKinley.

some view. Plan to bring your binoculars and spend some time here. You can go up some steel stairs and stand on the very top of Turquoise Mountain with a spectacular 360 degree view. It is a great place to have a picnic. At the foot of the peak there was a construction site that makes an ideal campsite.

Directions: Exit I-15 to the north at Halloran Springs Road. You're on a paved road and several dirt roads exit in different directions. Stay on the paved road. At 6.9 miles a dirt road goes left toward the peak. Continue on the paved road all the way to the top of the peak.
Coordinates: N35° 26' .142', W115° 55' .397', elevation 4510' ± 201'
Location: S&C DeLorme, page 70, A-2
Vehicle: 2WD

One of many antenna arrays on top of the peak.

You're likely to encounter many wild burros on the drive from Halloran Springs to the peak. Not only do they think they own the road—they do!

SUNSHINE IS GOOD
BUT
MOONSHINE IS
BETTER

APACHE CANYON MINES

Turquoise Mountain Area

While exploring the Turquoise Mountains, we looked down a steep mountainside and saw a lone miner working in a shallow pit. When we came within shouting distance, we asked him if it was okay to come down to where he was located. Sometimes people in remote areas like this don't like to have visitors. I was once greeted by a shot over the head with an old 30.06 rifle. That experience left me pretty gun shy. But this man was friendly and waved us down. He was pretty excited because he had just broken into some beautiful turquoise. Some of it was light colored and some was deep blue. We took some pictures of this turquoise still in place. He was generous and gave us some very good turquoise. It is said that the world's finest turquoise is mined here. He introduced himself as "Cochise" and said his partner was Ed Nazelrod. I had been looking for Ed because his name kept coming up as being very active in this area. It was said that he had a small gem store in Baker. Ed was at camp making jewelry. We

Above, spots of turquoise at the mine. Below, Ed Nazelrod left and Cochise on the right showing pieces of turquoise. All photos of this site by Don Taylor.

met him and he was packing a large gun but was very friendly. He showed us Indian tools he had found while mining turquoise and some of the jewelry he had made. It was very beautiful! He said people were free to camp and dig in the old dump for turquoise at no charge. Of course, he had plenty of gems for sale. All in all, we had a warm, friendly meeting.

You will be welcome especially if you share some of your provisions with Ed and Cochise. They are living in a very remote area and don't get to town very often. I felt I had taken a trip back in time of at least a hundred years. It was a wonderful experience. I told them I was writing a book and they welcomed the publicity.

Directions: Take the Halloran Springs exit to the north off I-15 NE of Baker. Re-set odometer. The road will fork several times but stay on the paved road. At 6.9 miles you reach a saddleback and the paved road continues up the mountain. Continue straight on the dirt road for 2.2 miles (9.1 miles total) keeping to the right every time the road forks.
Location: S&C DeLorme, page 70, A-2
Coordinates: N35° 26' 03", W115° 57' 20", elevation 3774'
Vehicle: 4WD

Artifacts found at the site and jewelry made from the turquoise mined here.

Yerba Mansa or Swamp Root (*anemopsis californica*). The leaves and roots of this plant were used for skin and joint problems, swelling, chest congestion, stomach ulcers and disinfecting cuts. Today it is used as a substitute for Golden Seal which is widely used by Native American practitioners.

CREE CAMP
and Hytens Well

Turquoise Mountain Area

High on a ridge in a deep canyon in the foothills of the Turquoise Mountains is a delightful little mining camp. There are several buildings in good shape complete with furniture and canned goods. The front yard shows the tender loving care of someone taking pride in their yard. The sides of the hill are carefully terraced and rock steps have been placed down the side of the hill. Several hundred yards up the canyon to the northeast are the well preserved ruins of a small milling operation. Everything was put together very carefully with large bolts. Behind the mill was a deep rock-lined well with water still in it.

Approach view of Cree Camp. All photos of this site by Sonny Hansen.

This camp shows that it was inhabited for a long period of time. Sadly, I have not been able to find out anything about this camp. I would appreciate any information about Cree Camp. If these hills could talk, what a story they could tell. Please don't disturb anything at this most interesting and mysterious place.

Hytens Well is actually two wells—one enclosed by wood on the north side and one enclosed by granite on the south side. The wooden well enclosure has collapsed but the granite one is intact with water in it. They are both hand dug at an old spring or seep because the vegetation shows that water is close to the surface. Be careful because the stone well is close to the road and is completely open. When I look down at it, I marvel at the amount of work it took to dig this well and line it with granite. Whoever did it did a beautiful job because it is in perfect condition. Who knows how many years it has been there. To the south a few feet is a small tailings pile proving that there had been a milling operation there at one time. Up to the west a trail goes over a hill and several prospect holes show signs of mining gold ore. The scenery is beautiful. What a story this canyon could tell if it could talk. I would love to have more information about this site and how it got the name of Hytens Well. It is interesting and mysterious—so still and quiet now.

View of the ore crusher.

Directions: From Baker (I-15 and SH127) go north on SH127 and turn right at .9 at power sub-station and travel on power-line access road. At

6.1 you will see a large nest in the steel tower supporting the power lines. At 8.1 take left fork. At 9.0 take right fork and continue to Cree Camp at approximately 10.6 miles. Hytens Well: Continue up the canyon to the left of Cree Camp and at 11.7 you will be at Hytens Well.

Location: S&C De Lorme, page 70, B-2
Coordinates: N35° 22' 31", W115° 57' 30", elevation 3055', (Hytens Well: N35° 22' 55", W115° 57' 30")
Vehicle: High clearance 2WD

Clockwise: living quarters and storage building, Hytens well—note wells on both sides of the road and two more views of the ore crusher.

ROSALIE

Valley Wells Area

Rosalie is a small ghost town that is slowly returning to the desert. The main reason for its existence was the discovery of the rich deposit of copper ore at the Copper World Mine high on the side of Clark Mountain. This discovery was made in the late 1860's or early 1870's but because of the remoteness, didn't boom until the turn of the century. In 1899, a large, fifty ton furnace was built to smelt and recover the copper. The United States was modernizing with electricity and there was a huge demand for copper. There were eighty-six men employed at the smelter and one hundred forty mules on the road between the mine and the smelter hauling copper ore. You can still see the double road in many places with one for uphill and the other for downhill. There was a post office and good accommodations for the miners. The miners homes can still be seen, dug out under a tufa cap behind the smelter. You must be careful not to drive on top of the tufa as it might collapse. The operation

Remains of the old Yates ranch house. All photos of this site by Ron McKinley.

doubled during World War I and closed when the war was over due to low prices. Some activity resulted when the price of copper rose at various times such as World War II but it is dormant now.

Rosalie also served as headquarters for the Yates Ranch from 1894 to 1952. It was the home of Boots and Bessie Yates. A huge area was grazed and Boots and his cowboys ranged over its extensive area. The Yates are both buried in the nearby cemetery. When I first discovered the Rosalie cemetery about twenty-five years ago, someone had placed an Indian metate as headstones on twenty or more unmarked graves. With the exception of one broken metate, they are all gone now. There is a white arrastré drag stone to the right of Bessie's and Boots' graves. The cemetery is fenced and in relatively good shape. The view of Clark Mountain towering to the north and the Cima Dome to the south are awesome. What a beautiful place to be placed to rest. Please let these pioneers rest in peace.

Rosalie or Valley Wells is slumbering now. It is a great place to camp and explore. I have Dennis Casebier to thank for much of this information.

One of the miner's underground home.

Directions: Take I-15 to Cima Road (Valley Wells off-ramp), turn north
over freeway. Go 1.7 miles and turn right on a well traveled road. At 1.8 miles you will be at adobe ruins which was the
Yates Ranch Headquarters and is also the site of Rosalie which is spread over a large area.
Location: S&C DeLorme, page 71, A-4
Coordinates: N35° 27' 58", W115° 40' 45", elevation 3704'
Vehicle: 2WD

View of the old ranch house with slag heap in the foreground.

Caves the miners lived in at Rosalie.

COPPER WORLD MINE

Valley Wells Area

The Copper World mine was discovered in the late 1860s. It is high on the side of Clark Mountain and is in piñon pines and junipers. Because the elevation is over 5,000 feet, the miners often had to contend with snow. At the mouth of the mine is a huge "glory hole"—a large hole in which many tons of high grade copper ore were removed.

On the face of the rock behind the glory hole are several areas of beautiful azurite and malachite. Also scattered around are boulders with patches of these two vivid colors. In fact, the last mining activity was for gem quality specimens of these two minerals.

Because of the remoteness of the mine, it didn't boom until the railroads were close enough to provide reliable, cheap transportation. The boom years were from the turn of the century until the end of World War I. Until recently, there was occasional activity.

The remains of a large mining camp is here for you to explore. Remember what Shortfuse says about climbing down old mine shafts. Don't! Stay alive by staying out! Close your eyes and try to imagine all the sights and sounds that once emanated from this camp.

View of huge rock cairn as you approach the mine. All photos of this site by Don Taylor.

Directions: Exit I-15 at Cima Road (Valley Wells off-ramp), turn north over the freeway. Go 1.7 miles and turn right onto a well-traveled road. At 1.8 miles, turn right. At 2.0 miles turn right at the black copper slag pile and large cottonwood tree. At 4.1 miles you pass a mystery cairn on your left. Follow the road around a sharp right turn and at 5.5 miles turn left on the power line road. At 5.8 miles take the left fork (look for my cairn) You will see the agave roasting pits at 7.3 miles (see next story). Continue up the road, ending at the mine at 8.0 miles. The mine is on the left and the camp buildings are on the right.
Location: S&C De Lorme, page 57, D-5
Coordinates: N35° 30'19", W115° 36' 04", elevation 5394'
Vehicle: High clearance 2WD

The Copper World Mine.

INDIAN AGAVE ROASTING PITS

Valley Wells Area

East of the road and south of the Copper World Mine you will see two doughnut-shaped piles of rocks about 20 to 25 feet in diameter. These rocks are limestone or dolomite and have been broken by being in a fire. These are Indian agave roasting pits. The ashes at these pits have been carbon dated to be from 200 to over 600 years old. They were primarily used to roast the agave which grows profusely in this area. The agave is in the yucca family and was an important food source for the Indians. They also used the fibers in the leaves in many ways. They roasted from April through the summer months. The Indians would select a site, then dig a large hole. In the hole they would build a large fire, then let it die down. They would throw the entire agave plant on the coals, complete with heart and stalk. They would bury the agave, build a fire on top, and let it burn all night and all the next day. After they dug it up, it was ready to eat or pound into powder for storing. This was done in the same spot year after year and the rings grew in size. I love to visualize how it must have been with all the Indians busily harvesting and roasting the agave. I have eaten roasted agave and can assure you that it isn't one of my favorite foods!

These remote sites are now quiet and lonely but once burst with activity. I love the story these sites tell and hope you do too.

Directions: Exit I-15 at Cima Road (Valley Wells off-ramp), turn left or north over the freeway and at 1.7 miles turn right on a well traveled road. At 1.8 turn right. At 2.0 turn right at the black copper slag pile and large cottonwood tree. At 4.1

Author standing on one of the agave roasting pits. All photos of this site by Don Taylor.

miles you pass a large, mystery cairn on your left. Follow the road around a sharp right turn and at 5.5 miles, turn left on the power line road. At 5.8 miles take the left fork and look for my cairns. You will be at the roasting pits at 7.3 miles. There are two pits, one above the other, 75 or 100 yards to your right or east of the road.

Location: S&C De Lorme, page 57, D-5

Coordinates: N35° 30' 13", W115° 36' 05", elevation 5,355'

Vehicle: High clearance 2WD

Snow around agave plants.

KOKOWEEF
The Lost River Of Gold At Kokoweef Mountain

Mountain Pass Area

I have heard the fascinating story of the "lost river of gold" at Kokoweef Mountains many times since I came to Barstow in 1950. The abbreviated story goes like this: early in this century three Indian brothers, while exploring limestone caverns deep in Kokoweef Mountain, discovered an underground river complete with fantastically rich placer gold in black sand. On the way out, one of the brothers was killed in an accident and the other brothers were not able to get his body out. For some reason, the other brothers never returned. Years later they told their story to a white man with whom they had become friends. This man, Earl Dorr, published an account of his explorations of the caves and the river of black sand filled with gold. It was published in the California Mining Journal around 1935. It created a sensation and the hunt was on and continues to this day. During the hunt, a large trove of ancient fossils was discovered and the San Bernardino County Museum was contacted. Bob Reynolds, county paleontologist, excavated literally millions of bones from the sediment. He says that some could be as old as ten thousand years.

Entrance to the Kokoweef mining camp. Photo by Ron McKinley.

Kokoweef Mountain is in the Ivanpah Range and the mining camp is in the 5,000 foot range and has a beautiful view in a scenic area. The camp has grown. A large group of volunteer treasure seekers come and go. Usually work

Looking down on the Kokoweef camp. Photo by Don Taylor.

occurs on weekends. They even have a newsletter. The group is friendly and is headed by North Las Vegas business-man Larry Hahn. His address is: 2908 E. Lake Mead Blvd., North Las Vegas, Nevada, 89030. To see the Carbonate King mine stop at the Kokoweef camp and get permission. Take the left fork for one mile.

What a story these mountains could tell if they could talk. This is a beautiful, mysterious and interesting area to explore.

Directions: Exit I-15 at Bailey Road (Mountain Pass) off-ramp across from the Molycorp mine and go south. The paved road turns to dirt after a mile or so but it's well-maintained. At 1.2 miles take the left fork. At 3.1 take the left fork. At 4.5 arrive at Kokoweef Mining Camp. This road is well marked with Kokoweef signs.
Location: S&C De Lorme, page 71, A-6
Coordinates: N35° 23' 55", W116° 19' 00", elevation 5,000' ±
Vehicle: 2WD

View of ore chute coming off the mountain. Photo by Ron McKinley.

View of mine entrance on the side of the mountain. Photo by Ron McKinley.

DINOSAUR TRACKWAY

Mountain Pass Area

High on the south side of the Mescal Mountains is a large deposit of beautiful, layered Aztec sandstone. It is mostly bright red with layers of cream colored sandstone mixed in. This deposit is across a small, colorful valley from Kokoweef Mountain and the Kokoweef Mining Camp where they are searching for the lost river of gold. This sandstone area is very similar to the red sandstone of Utah and Colorado except that it is harder and very beautifully layered. Sometime in the distant past, it has been mined extensively for building stone and flagstone. I would love to see where they used some of this rock because it is so beautiful. On the back side of the deposit are the ruins of an old gin pole quarry operation. The pole would pivot and the miners would attach a large chunk of rock to the "T" part, then it would swing back and load it on a truck to take to market.

This sandstone was laid down millions of years ago, one

Above, some of the spectacular scenery at the Dinosaur Trackway. Below, looking uphill at Don Putnam. Photos by Ron McKinley.

layer at a time, one layer each season, like the rings in a tree. This was during the age of dinosaurs and some of these animals left their tracks to be preserved for these many years. In one place, a dinosaur left a trail of tracks and hence, the name dinosaur trackway. Sadly, the paleontologists felt they had to cover these tracks to protect them from vandalism. So don't expect to see many tracks. What you will see besides spectacular, remote scenery, are smaller tracks of rodents and dog-size tracks complete with claw marks. I also saw leaf molds and spectacular dendrites. A dendrite looks like a fossil fern but is in reality a manganese stain. There are a few single tracks that appear to be those of the dinosaur. It is a beautiful place to explore, but collecting anything is strictly prohibited. Take plenty of pictures, leave your own tracks and remember to pack it in and pack it out.

Directions: From Kokoweef camp re-set odometer to zero and continue. At .2 miles take the right fork. At 1.4 miles you're there. Park and walk up the hill.
Location: S&C De Lorme, page 71, A-5
Coordinates: N35° 23' 55", W116° 19' 00", elevation 5,000' ±
Vehicle: 2WD except for the last mile which is 4WD—or you can hike the last mile.

The author checking the "gin pole" used by miners at the Trackway. Photo by Don Taylor.

Fossilized tracks of unidentified animals. Photo by Don Taylor.

One of the many dendrites in the area. Photo by Ron McKinley.

View of the "Mountain of Gold" at Kokoweef taken at the Dinosaur Trackway by Ron McKinley.

CARTOONS BY ROCKY

RILEY'S CAMP

Mountain Pass Area

Riley's Camp was the home of a fascinating, colorful prospector and miner. He was one of the many personalities that came "out of the hills" to our powder magazine in Barstow to occasionally buy explosives. Little did we know in 1951, when we were offered and accepted the Hercules explosive distributorship that we were going to meet so many delightful and interesting personalities. I enjoyed visiting with them and pumping them for all kinds of information about their area. They have enriched my life.

Riley's name was John Riley Bembry but he

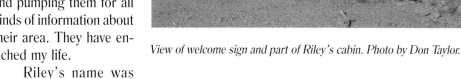

View of welcome sign and part of Riley's cabin. Photo by Don Taylor.

used the name of Riley. Riley was like a lot of prospectors of the time. He would share his last can of beans with you if you were hungry but would probably shoot you if you jumped one of his claims. He was an explosives expert and a veteran of World War I. He came to this area in the late 1920's from Los Angeles where he had been a meat-cutter and built his fascinating camp over the years. He filed on or bought over sixty mining claims in the area but made one big mistake. He didn't file a patent to get a deed on his camp until it was too late. He fought with the BLM but finally signed a "lifetime" agreement allowing him to live on the property until his death and then the land would revert to the government. He died January 7, 1984 and the BLM took control and the camp is now open to the public.

Riley's cabin. Photo by Don Taylor.

He lived in this camp over fifty years and there is considerable debris that is left from his era. Among the debris are his house, assay office, food cellar, and outhouse. Be sure to continue up the road to see his old riveted compressor that furnished air to his mine. The buildings are open and when you enter his home you will be shocked to see Riley sitting in the corner, greeting you with a sign-in sheet in his lap. Take special care with fire because these buildings are old and flammable. A great place to explore. Treat it with respect!

En-route to Riley's Camp, is a quaint, fenced cemetery where Riley and several of his friends are buried. It is in a beautiful Joshua Tree forest and I am sure they are resting in peace there. When he was buried, they stuck his pick, shovel, and gold pan in a cement cover over his grave. As of this date, most of the things are still there. Please let these hardy people rest in peace and show them respect. Thanks to Dennis Casebier for this information.

94

Directions: From Kokoweef, re-set odometer to zero and proceed 1.3 miles and take the left fork. At 2.1 take the right fork. At 4.3 take the left fork. At 5.3 take right fork. At 6.4 look to your left and you'll see a small grave site where Riley is buried. At 10.7 turn left. At 16.2 you'll pass an old, abandoned power shovel. At 16.8 continue straight and you can see Riley's camp from here. At 17.1 you're there.
Location: S&C DeLorme, page 71, B-6
Coordinates: N35° 21' .622', W115° 31' .038', elevation 3097±
Vehicle: High clearance 2WD

Figure of Riley set up by friends and relatives. Photo by Ron McKinley.

Riley's food cellar. Photo by Ron McKinley.

Riley's grave. Photo by Ron McKinley.

Leave Us Alone!

ABOUT THE AUTHOR

I was born in Kansas on Dec. 30, 1926 and moved to California in 1929. I have two brothers.

Once, my father was asked to temporarily take over an ailing Boy Scout troop. This "temporary" job turned out to be a life-long commitment. It introduced me to hiking and camping, but most importantly, to the Mojave Desert. All three boys and dad became Eagle Scouts. Scouting has really enhanced my life.

In June, 1944, I graduated from Pomona High School followed by service in the U.S. Merchant Marines for two years. In service, I had a "distinguished" career as a cook and baker on a small, grubby, assault ammunitions ship assigned to the Marine Corps. We made five landings to provide ammunition during the war and one after the war to Northern China. It was an experience that taught me to enjoy every day of life.

After the war, I returned to graduate with an A.A. from Mount San Antonio College. I then entered Pomona College in Claremont and graduated in 1952 with a B.A. in history. During this time, I prowled the desert, camping, exploring and prospecting.

After graduation from Pomona College, I co-founded with my cousin, Ron Brubaker, Brubaker-Mann, Inc.. It is a mining company that produces specialty rock products and now I am the sole owner and still involved with this company after forty-nine years.

Because of my life-long love of history and the desert, I served for twelve years on the San Bernardino County Museum Commission and as chairman of that board for two years. I also became a charter member of The Mojave River Valley Museum in Barstow, served two terms as president and was on the board for many years. I have led museum field trips for over twenty one years.

I am currently serving as Wild Life Representative on the San Bernardino County RIAC board—a board that relates to cattle grazing issues in the desert.

An avid camper in the desert for more than **fifty** years, I am a fierce protector of the desert. I am married to my best friend and have one son and four daughters.